Portland Renaissance

When Creativity Redefined a City

BARRY LOCKE

PUBLISHED BY:
Alden Corner Publishing
PORTLAND, OREGON

Alden Corner Publishing
Portland, Oregon

Printed in the United States.

For information, contact: BarryTLocke@gmail.com
www.Renaissancepdx.com

Hardcover ISBN: 979-8-9889385-0-7
Paperback ISBN: 979-8-9889385-1-4
ebook ISBN: 979-8-9889385-2-1
Library of Congress Control Number: 2023920261

Cover design by Billy Lymm

To Kim, my muse, my consigliere,
and easily the best of what I found in Portland.

Contents

Author's Note

The idea for this book came to me in 2022 while I was lying in a hospital bed after successful surgery for cancer. Clearing a major milestone in a battle against a life-threatening disease, I wondered what I should do next. It didn't take long for my thoughts to turn to Portland, the city I quickly fell in love with when I moved here in 1994. Portland was easy-going, friendly, and quirky. It was also bursting with creativity and individual ingenuity, much of which I would learn had taken hold within the previous 10 years, and would continue in the years to come. It is a time that deserves to be celebrated.

I interviewed almost 50 people for this story, all of whom agreed the 1980s and '90s was a special time in Portland's history. With the help of their memories as well as media accounts, I'm happy to tell about it. What isn't here is an equal examination of Portland's problems during the era. As in any city, there were plenty. That's not this book and I'm not that writer. Respectfully, I wanted to explore Portland's successes, accomplishments that drew national attention to the area, and a time that redefined this city. Enjoy.

Introduction
A Golden Era for Creativity

It might not be wise to proclaim a particular era in a city's his-tory the most significant, or most influential, or most creative. Too many factors, collections of events, and individual life experiences can make any such declaration feel inherently subjective.

That said, in my book — which this is — the period from the mid-1980s through the 1990s in Portland, Oregon, was the most significant, most influential, and most creative time in the city's modern history.

It was a time that saw Portland emerge from, take your pick, an unsophisticated West Coast afterthought overshadowed by Seattle and San Francisco, a haven for freaks and geeks in a place yet to fully embrace the civic virtues of being weird, or a rough port town transitioning from a timber-based economy to a widely recognized creative hub.

During those final years of the 20th century, Portlanders produced visionary advertising that won national awards and ignited the local creative industry. They helped launch the craft brewing industry, which redefined how Americans drink beer. They designed shoes and clothes that would establish Portland as the athletic wear capital of the world. They opened restaurants that rivaled those in much larger cities. And they transformed a decaying warehouse district into an exemplar for urban living. These are things that got Portland noticed, and still today, are what the city is known for.

To put it another way, Portland became Sneakertown, Beervana, a dining jewel, an advertising hotbed, and the city that works. It encompassed a time that *The Washington Post* said, "changed the city into a hipster haven and international tourist destination."

Locals can contemplate whether that's a good or bad thing next time they're sitting in traffic on the Marquam Bridge, but the fact remains that Portland in the '80s and '90s enjoyed a renaissance that would redefine the city. Creativity showed up not only in the arts, but in ideas for new businesses, public-private partnerships to spur growth, and an acceptance that encouraged individual pursuits. Over and over, Portlanders had ideas and found ways to make them happen.

"There was just a bit of a sense that you could come here and you could be anything," said Karen Brooks, a longtime Portland writer. "Or you could just be nothing in the sense that you didn't have to have a big career or strive for more. If you wanted to do something really cool or interesting, if you wanted to be in the government, or you wanted to be in a band, or you wanted to have a restaurant, or you just wanted to do something, you could do it here."

It wasn't always that way. For most of the country, the 1970s and into the '80s were a struggle, particularly in

America's cities. Recession, double-digit interest rates, and a tight labor market contributed to a pessimism that left young people questioning their future, including in Portland.

"In the '70s, nobody in their right minds would stay in Portland, Oregon," said architect Brad Cloepfil. "Every young person left. Downtown was dead. The place was dead. And so everyone left. And then, you know, all of a sudden things started happening."

The seeds for Portland's renaissance had been planted in the years before. The low cost of living enabled creative individuals to pursue passion projects such as experimental filmmaking, independent newspapers, community theater, music, and the like, while still making rent.

"There was a real underground creative community," said longtime Portland arts critic Bob Hicks. "A lot of people moved to Portland because it was cheap. You could be a poor artist without being a starving artist."

Politically, the tenor changed from backroom dealing to community involvement, which led to urban success stories like converting downtown streets into bus-only routes and the beginning of an extensive light rail system. A concerted desire to make downtown more livable produced a vast waterfront park and a central square. For whatever challenges Portland was undergoing, there was a spirit to make things better.

"To its credit, I think the city wanted this," said restaurant owner Cory Schreiber. "I mean, from every level that you're looking at, the arts, the sports, the radio, the journalism, the architecture, the urban planning, all that stuff. To me, it was always woven in together."

Over time, the economy improved and opportunity increased. Homegrown athletic wear companies saw their national profiles enhanced in part by the creativity of local ad agencies. Art galleries, restaurants, and beer pubs added to the city's enjoyment. People continued to pursue and enjoy their creative interests.

"Portland just became sort of a mecca," said Bill Foster, who ran Portland's Northwest Film Center from 1981 to 2018. "There was the ad agency business, the photography business, graphic design, musicians, writers. All these people plying their trade."

Many credit Portland's geography as a relatively secluded outpost for an anything-goes attitude that spurs creativity. Others point to the mountains and the coast as diversions and inspirations. Some even credit the weather for helping to nurture ideas.

"A lot of the year it's gray, so you have to add your own color," designer Steve Sandstrom said. "If you're in that gray environment, it's kind of neutral space for you to go and do something to brighten it, or darken it, or whatever. But it is sort of a blank canvas."

To be sure, Portland was not perfect. Known as the Whitest city in America, it had long incorporated policies that negatively impacted Black communities. A history of redlining — the practice of denying mortgage loans to non-Whites in certain areas — followed by redevelopment of neighborhoods in the inner core resulted in the displacement of Blacks from many neighborhoods, including Albina. White supremacists roamed the city and in 1988 beat to death an Ethiopian immigrant, which soon would earn

Portland the title of "Skinhead City." The LGBTQ community also was under attack, informally in a society largely often hostile to its members and formally in multiple ultimately unsuccessful statewide ballot measures seeking to deny their rights.

Yet positive word spread that something cool was happening in Portland, attracting young people who added their own contributions to the city even as longtime residents sought progress as well.

"It was a renaissance, culturally, civically, across the board," said visual artist and urban planner Tad Savinar. "People were willing to roll up their sleeves and forge ahead."

Any discussion of a renaissance touts the importance of self-determination and the inherent rewards of curiosity and individual pursuits. To be sure, Portland welcomed those pursuits and allowed them to take root, which in turn seeded more change well into the 21st century. It remains to be seen whether the city can solve the problems of the early 2020s — rising crime, drug use, mental health, and homelessness — with solutions that benefit all. Maybe a look back to the 1980s and '90s can provide inspiration.

"Portland to me was the coolest place to live and evolved into that by being open to new ideas and to different people," said Kristy Edmunds, who started the Portland Institute of Contemporary Art in 1995. "It felt like a place where if you wanted something to happen, you could make it happen."

So much happened. And a new city emerged.

1

An Invitation to All

ON APRIL 6, 1984, A crowd estimated at 10,000 gathered in downtown Portland for a celebration. In a scene to be repeated over the next several decades for causes and gatherings large and small, the opening of Pioneer Courthouse Square gave all who were there the opportunity to experience for the first time what architect Will Martin called "a downtown living room for the people of Portland."

Mayor Frank Ivancie, who had opposed the project, put his political spin on his remarks, saying, "Like any good family, the people of Portland join ranks and get the job done."

It took decades to get Pioneer Courthouse Square done. From a notion that began in the 1960s, took hold in the '70s, and culminated in the '80s, the goal was clear: Invite Portlanders downtown.

The idea for a major downtown public space that would become Pioneer Courthouse Square emerged in 1961. A one-block site, bound by Southwest Broadway, Salmon, Yamhill, and 6th Avenue, held a two-story parking lot where the elegant Portland Hotel once stood. With its central location, Mayor Terry Schrunk ordered city planners to study the site as a potential "focal point" for the city.

The effort was a recognition that downtown Portland needed an upgrade. Following the national trend, people had largely abandoned urban settings in favor of suburban living. That left a tired downtown, disproportionately inhabited by bars and strip clubs, in a city with a struggling economy.

At the same time, a new energy was emerging, creating more civic involvement and a desire for a better way of life.

"There was certainly a shift from the 'old guys in suits and hats' kind of politicians in the 1950s to the '70s," said Bill Foster, longtime director of Portland's Northwest Film Center. "I think it was just the idealism of the age, and the people moving here from other places. Neil Goldschmidt gets the credit for being the catalyst that shook off the old-fashioned city bureaucracy. I think he certainly inspired a bunch of people that came of age in the '60s that had a different attitude about life."

It is hard to reconcile the accomplishments of Goldschmidt, Portland's mayor from 1973-79, with the later accounts of his repeated sexual abuse of an underage girl while he was in office. But his influence in the revitalization of downtown, opening up city government to greater neighborhood representation, and drawing talented people to key city commissions, all contributed to a new realization of what Portland could be.

During the 1970s, Harbor Drive was removed to make room for a 35-acre riverfront park. It was renamed Tom McCall Waterfront Park in 1984 after the Oregon governor who initiated the project in the late-'60s. As Pioneer Courthouse Square became known as Portland's living room, Waterfront Park served as its front yard, playing host to festivals, concerts, speaking events, as well as sunbathers, runners, and casual guests for years to come.

In addition, the Portland Transit Mall, a public transportation corridor that opened in 1977, converted Northwest 5th and 6th Avenues to mostly bus traffic. Goldschmidt also led the revolt against the controversial Mount Hood Freeway proposal, which would have cut through neighborhoods in Southeast Portland. Instead, the money designated for the freeway helped fund MAX light rail, which opened in 1986.

Much of the thinking for the future of Portland was outlined in the 1972 Downtown Plan. Fifteen months in the making, the report, with contributions from a citizen advisory group, offered recommendations to "enhance the livability of downtown."

A key goal was to "develop a major city square in the center of downtown to provide a focal point and gathering place." The debate continued over what that would be and in 1980 the city staged an open design competition that drew 162 entries nationwide.

Finalists emerged from New York City, San Francisco/ Los Angeles, Boston, Philadelphia, and Portland, and were given $10,000 each to develop their pitch. The competition included Lawrence Halprin, who had designed Ghirardelli Square in San Francisco, and Warren Schwartz, designer of New York's City Hall.

Martin, the Portland architect, assembled a team of outside advisers, a sort of creative kitchen cabinet, to help develop and then critique ideas. Inspired by plazas in Europe, including the Piazza del Campo in Siena, Italy, they developed a plan for an open-air space that could accommodate virtually any type of public event.

"I'm intrigued with the idea of always leaving something for the observer to complete," Martin told *The Oregonian*.

As part of their blind entry, Martin and his team built an intricate hardwood model assembled in the basement of a former Buddhist temple at Northwest 10th Avenue and Everett Street.

"His theory was we couldn't tell them that we were from Portland, but we could show them that we had a sensibility and a caring for this project that no one else did," said Cameron Hyde, a young architect at Martin's firm. "Everybody in the whole office was really excited about it. And every time we had a lunch hour or before and after work, we'd go down and see what was going on."

When it came time to choose a winner, judges acknowledged the diversity of potential uses when they selected the proposal from Martin's group in the summer of 1980. It was a big idea, led by a big thinker.

"He was definitely a big-picture guy," Hyde said. "He couldn't detail anything at all. But he had a really good sense for what things should be. The idea of the public square I thought was right on."

Not everyone agreed. Powerful business interests, fearing the square would become a gathering spot for transients, preferred a glass-enclosed structure, perhaps even requiring admission. Private donations to fund the park dried up. Within just a few months of the competition, Mayor Ivancie declared the project dead.

Public outcry was immediate and loud. Former Governor McCall, still a powerful voice through his weekly television commentary, blasted the potential rejection of the design competition's result. One Saturday, Martin led his agency's workers to the site. Using bright orange paint over the one-square-block area, they painted the entire surface to show what the square would look like. Soon, a citizens' group conceived the idea to sell personalized bricks to the public to help overcome the budget shortfall.

In a sign of a new era, public sentiment won out. The city got its square.

According to *The Oregonian*, many in the crowd spent their time ahead of the noontime opening ceremony searching among the 60,000 personalized bricks that covered the square's lower arena. Sold to the public for $15 or $30, the bricks contributed to the 30 percent of the $7.9 million project that was privately financed.

"The family feud is over," Martin declared during the ceremony, sailing his flat-brimmed hat into the crowd. It was his 54th birthday.

The square's multiple levels of steps doubled as seating in an amphitheater-type setting, and one corner included wrought-iron fencing saved from the Portland Hotel. In its first year, the square played host to a break-dancing

Thousands fill Pioneer Courthouse Square at its opening ceremony in 1984. (City of Portland (OR) Archives, AP/7881)

contest attended by thousands, the Olympic Torch Relay in advance of the upcoming Summer Games in Los Angeles, and the first annual Christmas tree-lighting ceremony. *Time* magazine called it one of the top 10 design achievements of 1984. Since then, the square has often played host to more than 300 events a year, definitely living up to its goal of becoming Portland's living room.

Thirty years after it opened, a member of Martin's team reflected on the accomplishment.

"It's that Joni Mitchell song, only in reverse," landscape architect J. Douglas Macy told *The Oregonian*. "We tore up a parking lot and put up paradise."

Pioneer Courthouse Square was one of several projects completed around the same time, all of which combined to change Portland's downtown. The iconic KOIN Center, a business and residential tower, also opened in 1984. The same year, the Paramount Theater on Southwest Broadway was renovated and reopened as the Arlene Schnitzer Concert Hall, named for the influential patron of the Portland art scene. Next door, the Heathman Hotel was renovated at the same time, returning the 1927 building to its elegant past and providing yet more proof of new life for downtown.

A year earlier, the U.S. Bancorp Tower, also known as Big Pink, opened at Southwest 5th Avenue and Pine Street. And in 1985, Portlandia, the largest copper repousse statue in the United States besides the Statue of Liberty, arrived on a barge on the Willamette River and found a home at the Portland Building at Southwest 5th Avenue and Main Street.

As evidenced by the downtown revival, Portland was coming out of the economic doldrums of the late '70s and early '80s with shared optimism, moving into an era of growth creatively, culturally, and commercially.

It was time for a renaissance.

And another thing…

Just 17 months after it opened, Pioneer Courthouse Square would prove capable of playing host to somber occasions. Will Martin, 55, died when the plane he was flying crashed in the Grand Canyon. On October 13, 1985, a crowd of 500 mourned Martin and his son, 25-year-old Eric, who also died in the crash.

Portland Mayor Bud Clark, who started the first of his two terms 10 months earlier, said Martin "chose to regard human life as a celebration and not a series of trials."

Martin took enormous pride in Pioneer Courthouse Square, visiting often in the months after its completion with his wife, Gail. "He just thrilled to see it used in the way it was envisioned," she told the crowd. "He loved the square and would have been so honored by the tribute you pay him."

2

Portland Gets Its Star

THE 1984 NBA DRAFT IS most notable for two things: The Chicago Bull drafted Michael Jordan and the Portland Trail Blazers didn't.

Decades later, the explanation remains. After Houston drafted future Hall of Fame center Akeem (later Hakeem) Olajuwon, the Blazers chose second. Portland already had another future Hall of Famer, Clyde Drexler, selected the year before, at Jordan's position of shooting guard. Portland needed a center.

"So play him at center," Bobby Knight urged Blazers general manager Stu Inman. Knight, Jordan's coach on the U.S. Olympic team that summer, was that certain about Jordan's NBA future.

Instead, the Blazers selected Sam Bowie. A 7-foot center, Bowie missed two full seasons in college recovering from a fractured left tibia. During his four seasons in Portland, injuries allowed him to play in more than half the Blazers' games only once. By Bowie's last professional season in 1994-95, Jordan had won three NBA Championships and would win three more.

Although the Blazers missed their opportunity for Jordan, Portland did not. In fact, his association with the town would last long beyond his playing days and he would have a major impact on the success of two prominent local companies, Nike and Wieden+Kennedy.

Nike did not have the luxury of selecting Jordan from a draft of college players. When it came to the shoe companies, he was a free agent, and Nike, coming off the first quarter of declining revenues in its history in 1983, went all in.

Accounts vary over the amount of credit that should go to individuals, but drawing from multiple newspaper and magazine stories, the pursuit played out something like this:

One of the assistant coaches on the '84 Olympic team, George Raveling, befriended Jordan. Raveling, then a Nike-sponsored coach at Iowa State, constantly urged Jordan to consider Nike.

Nike marketing head Rob Strasser, whose legal background made him more of a deal-making expert than a basketball savant, recognized where the future of sports marketing was going. He wanted a singular icon to help build Nike's basketball business.

"Individual athletes, even more than teams, will be the heroes," he wrote in a 1983 memo. "(They'll be) symbols more and more of what real people can't do anymore — risk and win."

Given that, Sonny Vaccaro, Nike's in-house college bas-ketball expert, lobbied co-founder Phil Knight and Strasser to go after Jordan hard.

Strasser and designer Peter Moore met with Jordan's agent, David Falk, who sought a commitment for a signa-ture shoe and apparel line, advertising, and a percentage of sales. When discussions turned to what Jordan's product line should be called, Falk eventually suggested Air Jordan, perfectly capturing the synergy between the high-flying athlete and the Nike Air cushioning that had been intro-duced in running shoes.

Nike would offer Jordan a percentage of product sales, a record $2.5 million over five years, and a commitment to market Jordan like no other brand would. The biggest issue was getting Jordan, who wore Converse during games at North Carolina and Adidas whenever he could, to consider Nike. Urged by Falk, Jordan's parents were instrumental in getting him to take the Nike meeting in Beaverton.

"My mother said, 'You're gonna go listen. You may not like it, but you're gonna go listen,'" Jordan said in "The Last Dance" documentary series. "She made me get on that plane and go listen."

What Jordan and his parents saw was a full-court presentation that showed Nike's commitment to the young star.

"I absolutely fell in love (with Strasser) when he actual-ly made the first presentation of the Jordan thing, the Air Jordan concept," Jordan told *USA Today* in 2015.

Converse was the traditional leader in basketball shoes with a large stable of endorsees, including Larry Bird,

Magic Johnson, and Julius Erving. There was no plan to place Jordan atop their marketing pyramid.

Another brand, Spot-Bilt, reportedly made a strong financial play on the advice of its vice president of promotions, O.J. Simpson. Jason Hehir, the director of the Jordan documentary series, "The Last Dance," told the story on an aftershow following Episode 5, saying "He (Simpson) said to the guys at Spot-Bilt 'The kid out of Carolina is the next me. Go get him.'" The offer came, but the brand was unable to match Nike's commitment to marketing Jordan.

Adidas, Jordan's first choice, was struggling and unable to commit either the money or signature product for Jordan. When the company balked at Jordan's plea to match Nike's offer, the deal was done.

The 2023 movie *Air* brought new attention to the Jordan-to-Nike story, and plenty of debate over who was most responsible. The film gives a large amount of credit to Vaccaro, played by Matt Damon. Director Ben Affleck, who also played Knight in the movie, cautioned against taking the story too literally.

"This is not a documentary," he told an approving audience at the film's premiere at the South by Southwest festival in Austin, Texas. "This is not meant to be the absolute perfect history of who did what and who said what."

It certainly makes sense that in the decision to pursue Jordan, Vaccaro's voice was the loudest. Working for Nike since the late-1970s, he built relationships with dozens of college coaches who were paid to put their teams exclusively in Nike shoes. He knew the game and its emerging stars.

Of course, singling out Jordan could not have been too much of a reach, as he was *The Sporting News* National Player of the Years for two years running when he left North Carolina for the NBA. Strasser, who had a strong relationship with Falk, drove the deal and laid out its advantages to Jordan.

"Sonny didn't influence me to go to Nike. He got a deal proposed," Jordan said.

Vaccaro admitted after *Air* came out that he never went to Jordan's parents' house as shown in the movie. And Knight told Affleck that it was Strasser, not Vaccaro, who made the pivotal speech during the presentation to Jordan. Still, in the same *USA Today* story in which Jordan credited Raveling and Strasser, Moore said Vaccaro's contribution was second only to Strasser's.

"This whole episode is very typical of Nike history. You get a slightly different story from everyone you talk to," said Moore, Nike's first creative director. "Sonny was the second MVP in the deal. He picked Jordan out of all those kids that played basketball in college."

The marriage succeeded from the start. In the NBA pre-season, Jordan took the court in red-and-black shoes, running afoul of the NBA's uniform standards that shoes be mostly white. With the threat of the NBA issuing progressively larger fines for every game Jordan broke the rule, lore has it that Strasser welcomed the penalty. In fact, Nike released a commercial to maximize the publicity.

The spot, titled "Banned," opens with a shot of Jordan handling a basketball. As the camera angle moves from the rookie's face downward, a voiceover delivers the message:

"On September 15th, Nike created a revolutionary new basketball shoe. On October 18th, the NBA threw them out of the game. Fortunately, the NBA can't stop you from wearing them. Air Jordans. From Nike."

A clanging sound follows and a black box covers each of the shoes. The Jordan logo, designed by Moore and inspired by a pilot's wings, closes the spot.

Jordan would win the NBA Rookie of the Year Award, averaging 28.2 points per game. Air Jordan, projected to generate $3 million in revenue over its first three years, sold a reported $163 million in its first year and was well on its way to becoming a $6 billion a year brand. And in due time, Wieden+Kennedy's commercials featuring Jordan would help propel the Portland ad agency to the top of the industry.

As for the Trail Blazers? Sam Bowie averaged 10 points per game as a rookie and would never play a full season for Portland again.

And another thing...

The first Nike shoes Michael Jordan wore in the NBA were not Air Jordans. With little time to create Jordan's signature shoe after he chose Nike weeks before his first training camp, the company delivered an existing model, the Air Ship. He wore the red-and-black colorway in an exhibition on Oct. 18, 1984, defying NBA standards for shoe colors.

But there is no record of him wearing them in a regular-season game, or actually receiving a fine. He wore Air Ships, in a mostly white colorway, to start the season.

In his 11th NBA game, on November 17, 1984, Jordan played in Air Jordans for the first time. He reportedly went back to the Air Ship and wore Jordans again on December 20. The shoe was released to the public early the next year, starting a sports and culture phenomenon that still thrives.

3

One Tough Campaign

AROUND THE SAME TIME NIKE was wooing Michael Jordan, the most important brand endorser in its history, Columbia Sportswear found its advertising icon in-house. Gert Boyle, the chairwoman of the board, also became the star in a long-running series of print ads that helped propel the outerwear brand from $18 million to $100 million in sales by the end of the 1980s. With television added to the campaign in the '90s, sales jumped to more than $350 million by 1997.

"One Tough Mother" was conceived and developed by Portland ad agency Borders, Perrin & Norrander. An earlier campaign focused on technical benefits, but as the market became more competitive with larger companies, the agency and its client sought a way to differentiate. The solution came by featuring Gert and her son, Tim Boyle, Columbia's president.

Ads featuring Gert Boyle helped lift Columbia Sportswear's fortunes. (Image courtesy of Bill Borders)

"Then it became an anti-giant clothing designer position, and what better way to do that than to personalize the company," said BPN co-founder and creative director Bill Borders. "As we'd have more meetings with Tim and Gert, with their personalities, we'd come back and talk about them. We didn't really think about it being a campaign at the time. But we got to that once we both decided that we needed a new direction."

"One Tough Mother" featured Gert Boyle, 60 when the campaign began, as the gruff, demanding product perfectionist. Tim was the comic foil in the TV spots, wear-testing Columbia outdoor clothing. There was Tim, walking through a car wash. Or getting dropped off by helicopter atop a snow-covered mountain. There he was again, beneath the surface of an ice rink as Gert drove a Zamboni ice-grooming machine over him. The tagline announced, "Tested. Tough."

In her 2005 book, *One Tough Mother*, Gert Boyle said, "The impact of the ads was almost instantaneous. Sales quickly increased, and I was surprised when strangers came up to me on the streets and asked if I was the Tough Mother."

The ads were quirky, informative, and most of all, authentic. The Columbia story began in 1937 when Gert's parents moved the family from Nazi Germany to Portland and bought a small hat company. Columbia added outerwear in the 1950s and Paul Lamfrom, Gert's father, ran the company until his death in 1964. Gert's husband, Neal Boyle, assumed leadership, but when Neal died of a heart attack in 1970, Gert and Tim, who at the time was a student at the University of Oregon, took over and kept the struggling company alive.

Columbia was generating a reported $650,000 in sales when Gert tried to sell the company. When a proposed deal would net her only $1,400, she became determined to tough it out. That toughness became the defining tone of the company's most-successful campaign.

"It was real," Borders said. "Gert sat in on the meetings and she really did kind of rule the place with a velvet iron fist. She had her hands in everything. She sometimes drove Tim crazy, but there was a lot of love there. It was perfect, it really was."

One early print ad featured an introduction to Gert by Tim, differentiating Columbia from larger rivals. "See, to say mom kind of takes our product quality serious is like saying Vince Lombardi kind of took football serious," it read. The headline of another ad announced, "Yet another innovation from a woman who refuses to grow old gracefully." The phone number to find the nearest dealer was 1-800-MA-BOYLE.

"It basically said this is a big, family-run company that cares about the product quality, and it comes through if you do it with a smile," Borders said. He added that Tim made a key recommendation to not include pricing in product ads, even though Columbia usually was priced much less than high-end outdoor clothiers such as North Face and Patagonia. "He said 'No, let's let the consumers discover that and be pleasantly surprised at the point of sale.'"

Borders came to Portland from Southern California in the early 1970s and was immediately struck by two things: the natural beauty of the area, and the lack of quality at most of the ad agencies. In fact, interviews at the first four firms he visited had him rethinking his decision.

"I went from really loving the town and just the environment to being disappointed by the work that I saw," he said. "A lot of people didn't understand my portfolio. They didn't get it creatively. And I looked at their work on the walls and I realized it probably wasn't going to be a good fit. I thought I wasn't going to move here."

His fifth interview changed everything. He connected immediately with John Brown, the creative director at Cole & Weber, and went to work.

Over the next four years, Borders worked with art director Mark Norrander and account manager Wes Perrin at the Northwest's top ad agency. But when national powerhouse Ogilvy & Mather bought Cole & Weber in 1977, the trio opted to stay independent and open their own shop. Important clients would include Port of Portland, Burgerville, and Columbia.

"Fast forward just a couple of years," Borders said. "You had Wieden+Kennedy, which really helped blow it up. There was a whole recognition that you don't have to be in Los Angeles or San Francisco or New York for great advertising."

Portland's reputation grew and business increased, attracting talented creatives seeking a simpler lifestyle than the big cities offered. From humble beginnings, the industry flourished.

BPN grew to more than 100 employees, with offices in Portland and Seattle. Along the way, it gained a reputation for originality and a fierce commitment to quality. The agency's first ad in the Yellow Pages made it clear by stating, "Timid advertisers need not call."

"Before anything is the work and that sounds really basic," Borders said. "But if you do that, then other questions become easier."

Expectations grew during the "One Tough Mother" campaign, as each commercial was a chance to see what Gert and Tim were up to next. After a 20-year run, followed by a nearly 10-year break, Gert Boyle returned to a starring role in Columbia advertising in 2015 until her death in 2019 at age 95. By then, Columbia had grown to a $3 billion company, and Portland's advertising community had blossomed.

4

Something's Brewing

KARL OCKERT WAS CONCERNED. LABORING to open the only micro-brewery in Portland in 1984, the young brewmaster for what would soon be called Bridgeport got wind that a second brewery, Widmer Brewing, was also in the works.

"I thought, 'Crap, we're going to screw things up,'" he said. "There's no way in hell Portland can actually support more than one brewery. It's not going to happen."

He needn't have worried. Over the next 25 years, Portland's craft brewing industry would overflow with enthusiastic makers and beer drinkers alike. At various times, Portland has laid claim to having more breweries than any city in the world.

You'd be hard-pressed to find an industry utilizing more creativity in solving problems than Portland's nascent craft brewing efforts in the 1980s. From finding space to brew, jerry-rigging systems when specific brewing equipment didn't exist, getting people to accept new, more robust beers, to changing the law that allowed them to invite the public in, early brewers were constantly figuring out things on the fly. It seemed that experimenting with new styles and flavors of beer was the easy part, as the DIY spirit overflowed.

Bridgeport, initially called Columbia River Brewery, set up in the oldest industrial building in Portland, a former rope factory built in 1876 at Northwest Marshall Street and 13th Avenue. A block away, at Northwest Lovejoy and 14th, Widmer Brewing moved in. Six blocks south a third brewery, Portland Brewing, would also open at Northwest Flanders and 14th.

Ockert called it the scary warehouse district. Today it's known as the Pearl District.

It wasn't hard to understand the attraction to the run-down industrial area: cheap rent. Bridgeport's owners, Dick and Nancy Ponzi, who already ran a successful winery about 20 miles southwest of Portland, secured their 6,000-square-foot space for $600 a month.

Another factor was the area's history. Portland already had proven itself as a beer market by the time these new breweries were shopping for homes. Henry Weinhard, which began in the 1850s, was still operating at Northwest Burnside and 12th. Regulations in the area around it proved attractive to the small brewers.

"It was the only zone in Portland where you could put a brewery without a conditional use permit," Portland Brewing co-founder Fred Bowman said in a 2015 interview. "It worked out in our favor in other ways too. It was handy when one of us would run low on supplies. Often times we could go down the street and borrow whatever we needed from the other guy."

Learning how to build a brewing operation was a challenge for all.

"There was nobody selling equipment to small breweries. That just didn't exist," Ockert said, so they repurposed old dairy tanks from the Ponzis' winery. "We were walking Swiss Army knives. We had to do plumbing, electrical, framing, all the process piping, and whatever else we were putting together, we built by hand. "

Oregon's first true craft brewery, Cartwright Brewing, opened in 1979. Founder Chuck Coury owned his own winery in Forest Grove for 15 years, but his brewery lasted only two. His beer was doomed by a lack of consistency, as his brewing process provided a blueprint of how not to do it for those who followed. But one other thing was clear.

"We also saw how much Portland beer drinkers wanted him to succeed," Kurt Widmer said in 2014.

The market was primed. Henry Weinhard's Private Reserve had long provided a richer, more-flavorful alternative to ever-present mass producers Budweiser, Miller, and others. Local bars like the Produce Row Café and the Horse Brass Pub specialized in more interesting beers, including imports from the U.K., Germany, and beyond.

It was up to the new breweries to tap into Portland's affinity for all things new and different by convincing bar owners to sell their beer at a higher price than the large industrial brands. The Widmers, Kurt and his brother Rob, juiced enthusiasm with the "Widmer Designated Drinker" program, transporting friends to bars around town to order Widmer beer on draft.

With their opportunities limited to selling kegs to taverns, Bridgeport, Widmer, and the yet-to-launch Portland Brewing all wanted to sell directly to consumers, one pint at a time. They were joined by the McMenamin brothers, Mike and Brian, who already had a few pub-style restaurants around town, but had yet to make their own beer. Their goal seemed simple enough: to open pubs that offered food and homegrown beer.

Except that it was illegal. Oregon law did not allow brewers to make and serve beer on the same premises.

The pioneers of Portland's craft brewing industry merely faced the issue the same way they handled building their breweries or educating consumers: head on. They set out to get a new law in the state legislature, with frequent trips to Salem to lobby for the bill.

"Thank God Dick and Nancy Ponzi were with us because they had done it before with the wineries 10 years earlier," Brian McMenamin said. "So they were familiar with how the system worked. We were novices and young punks that didn't know any better."

The original bill passed the Oregon House, but was tabled in a Senate committee and died under pressure from large beer wholesalers. Another bill made it through the legislature and on July 13, 1985, Governor Vic Atiyeh signed Senate Bill 813. Known as the "Brewpub Bill," it created a brewery-public house license for manufacturers producing fewer than 25,000 barrels of malt beverage, and allowed retail sales.

It was a major step forward for Portland's beer scene.

"The Brewpub Bill brought craft beer out of the closet," Mike McMenamin told *Willamette Week* in 2015. "Once we had it, the whole idea of dark, dingy taverns started to slowly disappear. It got families in there and just opened things up."

McMenamin's Hillsdale Brewery and Public House became Oregon's first brewpub since Prohibition when it offered its own beer in October 1985. Bridgeport opened its pub early the next year.

"So they were the first to put a brewery into a pub, and we were the first to put a pub into a brewery," Bridgeport's Ockert pointed out.

Soon Bridgeport was offering pizza with fresh dough made with the wort of fermented beer.

"We were probably as well known for our pizza as the beer," Ockert said. "We had this little Easy-Bake oven pizza maker that did one pie at a time. It was kind of like the fish in a pond when you put the food pellets in. People would all just start racing to the bar to get their slice of pizza."

Meanwhile, Portland Brewing was trying to start operations and open its own pub in a building shared with already-existing Bogart's restaurant. Bowman, an avid home brewer along with co-founders Art Larrance and Jim Goodwin, had been researching for years.

"We had to figure out a way to finance it and by the time we got that we were the third one to get started," Bowman said in a 2015 oral history interview. "But it actually made it easier to grow when there were three (breweries) out there doing this, knocking on doors, selling locally produced beer, rather than just one. Because then it was a movement."

The size of the Portland Brewing space produced a challenge to open a family-friendly pub, as an inspector from the Oregon Liquor Control Commission determined a lack of separation between the bar and eating area was not appropriate for children.

Thinking quickly and creatively, Bowman made his case.

"I said, 'We think this thing is going to have a certain amount of attraction for tourists, and we don't want people to have to leave their kids out on the sidewalk to come in here. It's too bad you don't have a qualification that says minors are only allowed in the company of their parents because that's all I'm asking for.' He said, 'Well we don't have that qualification, but if you want to put that on the door, I'll okay the whole thing.'"

Such door signage quickly became standard practice.

Meanwhile, the Widmer brothers created the breakthrough beer of those early years. The industry's first American-style Hefeweizen also would become Portland's most commercially successful craft beer.

Kurt Widmer lived in Germany during the 1970s and brought his knowledge and enthusiasm for German beer home to Portland, where he and his brother Rob enjoyed home brewing. As Kurt Widmer described in an oral history, it was "a hobby that went out of control."

With the help of their father, Raymond, they created the Widmer Brewing Company, later renamed Widmer Brothers. Committing their own money and that of family members, they worked as long as 16 hours a day in the beginning. As Kurt Widmer said, "there was no Plan B."

Widmer's first two beers, an Altbier and a Weizenbier, proved popular. In fact, the Weizenbier, a filtered wheat beer, prompted the owners of the Dublin Pub on Southeast Hawthorne Boulevard to seek another like it. With both their fermenting tanks occupied by the first two beers, the brothers decided to attempt a non-filtered version with Cascade hops.

The resulting cloudy beer was a departure from what beer drinkers were used to, as was the wedge of lemon accompanying each draft pint. But Widmer Hefeweizen was a hit.

Those early years set the blueprint for Portland, with brewers experimenting with various styles and flavors of beer to a willing audience. Bridgeport created Bridgeport Ale and Blue Heron Ale, McMenamins came up with Hammerhead Ale, Ruby Ale, and Terminator Stout, and Portland Brewing offered Portland Ale, and later, MacTarnahan's Ale.

Inevitably, Portland would become famous for its love of craft beer and its pub culture.

"You could argue the birth of craft brewing was maybe Northern California, or somewhere else in the U.S.," Rob Widmer said in 2014. "But it's flourished here like no other place in the world."

······ 5 ······

An Appetite for Change

YOU DON'T BICYCLE ACROSS THE country without a curiosity for each place you'll see. How it reveals itself. What's unique about it. What it might be like to live there.

So when Greg Higgins pedaled west from New York in the late 1970s and made a stop in Portland, he took notice.

"I just liked the feel of it," he said. "Coming from where I grew up in Buffalo, which was a dying city at that time, just everything appealed to me about it."

The young chef moved to the Northwest, working first in Seattle, before taking over the kitchen in the revamped Heathman Hotel on Southwest Broadway in 1984. He saw a city waiting to take off.

"All the building blocks were here," Higgins said. "But it seemed like it was kind of behind the times."

To put it mildly.

Another transplant to Portland in the early 1980s, Karen Brooks began a long career as a restaurant critic in a town that had plenty of restaurants to be critical of.

"The restaurants, by and large, were pretty terrible. There was no scene to speak of," said Brooks, who arrived from Chicago. "If you look at some of my early reviews, the restaurants were like Saturday Night Live parodies of restaurants. A lot of them were like that, not all of them."

But the potential was there, in and around Portland, sprouting from the ground, swimming in rivers, and growing on trees.

"It was just world-class ingredients," Brooks said. "Some of the best you'll find really anywhere on the planet."

In her book *Oregon's Cuisine of the Rain*, Brooks provides an alternative to the cuisine of the sun, the nickname for Mediterranean food from warm climates such as southern France, Italy, and Greece. In Oregon, the rain creates the rich soil and lush forests conducive to abundant and flavorful ingredients.

"The rain gives us our soul, our sense of place," she writes. "It also gives us endless raw materials for fashioning a whole new way of cooking."

From produce, herbs, and mushrooms to oysters, salmon, and sturgeon, to berries, nuts, and figs, Oregon's bounty offered a limitless palette for creative chefs to express themselves with variations on traditional dishes or entirely new offerings.

"There's no place that I've been that can rival Portland for the quality and diversity of ingredients," Higgins said. "So as a chef that's really special to me."

Higgins was one of the first chefs to take full advantage of Portland's urban growth boundary. Established in the 1970s, Oregon's land-use regulations were adopted to preserve farmlands and prevent urban sprawl. The resulting proximity to nature benefits not only Portland's citizenry, but also its chefs. A decade before opening his eponymous restaurant, Higgins worked on building a supply network that would help define his farm-to-table approach.

"In my free time, I would bike out in the country, all the way out to, you name it, McMinnville and further, and if I saw a cool operation, I'd stop and talk with people and start recruiting people," he said. "I'd say if your neighbors are growing, what are they growing? Are they interested? Do you want to bring some of their stuff? And so we built those relationships like that."

Some of the relationships were forged closer to home, or in Higgins' case, work.

"There was this gal, kind of a hippie gal, taking care of the plants in the lobby at the Heathman, the palm trees and all that," he said. "So I just chatted with her when I was getting a cup of coffee early one morning. She was in there watering the plants, and I was like, 'Oh, you like plants?' And she says, 'Oh, yeah, I have a little place out in Canby.' I assumed it was just ornamentals and flowers. And she says, 'No, I grow some herbs and stuff like that.' I said, 'Well, do you want to bring some herbs for me?' So we started this thing going with her and she started bringing herbs. Then the operation grew and she started buying from her neighbors and bringing them in."

In a short time, the Heathman became one of Portland's favorite restaurants. In naming it *The Oregonian's* Restaurant of the Year in 1988, Brooks wrote that chefs Higgins and George Tate "have transformed a den of disaster into a showcase of regional excellence." It showed that Portland diners could move away from what they had known and appreciate seasonal food that came from their own backyard.

"Even though I thought the food scene here was kind of dated for that period, there were still people who were really receptive to certain things like forest mushrooms, and game meats, and really good seafood," Higgins said. "For a chef, that's what you build your kitchen on."

It was also an example of the type of DIY self-determination — a chef at a high-end hotel creating his own food supply chain — that would mark the 1980s. Portland proved an incubator for non-traditional ideas, many of which inspired the adventurous excellence of Portland restaurants in the 21st century. It happened quietly, without the scrutiny one might find in San Francisco or Seattle, where costs — and expectations — were higher.

"There were no judgments on Portland. No one cared," Brooks said. "I think that turned out to be a great thing. It was like having your parents out of town."

It's why, Brooks said, a regular at L'Auberge might be presented with a covered plate at dessert, only to find a joint inside. It's why the owners of Vat and Tonsure, a downtown favorite, could get away with refusing to turn down the opera music they loved. And it's what let caterers Nancy Briggs and Juanita Crampton think they could offer

Table for Two, a lunch restaurant that welcomed only two people and a months-long wait for reservations.

"There was a little bit of a sense of lawlessness and chaos that, as the scene kind of started percolating, made it really fun," Brooks said.

Other restaurants influenced Portland dining behavior for future generations. Michael Vidor, who started both L'Auberge on West Burnside and Genoa on Southeast Belmont, welcomed a less-dressy, jeans-permitted approach even in high-end restaurants. Genoa, which opened in 1971 with a menu boasting a seven-course Italian meal for $7, showed the farm-to-table ethos with its commitment to local ingredients. And Millie Howe, owner of Indigene near Southeast 37th Avenue and Division Street, was perhaps the first to make weekend brunch an appointment to savor, complete with communal tables.

While the spotlight shone brighter elsewhere, Portland dining was not completely in the dark to out-of-towners. In 1986, one writer got a taste of enough that was good to make a prediction for the future.

"Restaurants do not shine in Portland. There is none of the cult madness afflicting the other Pacific Coast cities," Lois Dwan wrote in the *Los Angeles Times*. "There are glimmers, however small, but strengthening. Tiny restaurants, muffled in odd locations, have steadied to the point where reservations can be difficult. They are mostly chef-owned and the chefs are skilled and aware of what is happening elsewhere. A culinary academy has been established. I suspect the isolation is about to end."

······ **6** ······

Art is On the Move

YOU CAN'T HAVE A RENAISSANCE without art. In the 1980s, Portland's art scene was undergoing a transition, one that produced accessibility and exposure for artists, opportunities for collectors and casual observers, and a strong linkage to what would one day become the Pearl District.

"It wasn't really much of an art scene. If you came out of a bigger city, you had to really work to find it," said Elizabeth Leach, who opened her gallery for contemporary art in 1981. "I think it was all very small and kind of supportive, but on a very low-key basis."

So, mirroring what many Portlanders of the era were doing, Leach took matters into her own hands. Accustomed to the art scene in Los Angeles, New York, and Paris, she opened her own gallery with the goal of bringing the works of national artists to Portland, and exporting regional art beyond the Northwest. She networked religiously, built a following through cold-calling local businesses, and started a rental program for contemporary art pieces.

"There was a real interest in the corporations having art in their lobbies, having art on their walls," she said. "So the businesses supported me originally."

Leach got a big break in 1984 when she was selected to curate a collection for the Heathman Hotel, which was being renovated into a high-end, downtown destination. By recommending and collecting works by pop artists Andy Warhol and Wayne Thiebaud in common spaces, and regional artists in rooms, she was responsible for much of the hotel's feel.

"So that gave me a stamp of approval because I was 24 when I opened my gallery," she said. "I had individuals who were advocates for me as a woman-owned business and me as a gallery. It was slow, but it grew. And there was a lot of support."

From 1961 to 1986, Arlene Schnitzer's Fountain Gallery had a firm hold on the Portland art scene. Dubbed the city's first serious art gallery, it focused on providing a platform to Northwest artists even when opportunities to expand its reach to the national scene emerged.

"God, when I think about it," Schnitzer told *Portland Monthly* in 2012, "I could have had a Warhol Campbell's soup can for $50, the flowers and Maos for $1,200. But I couldn't do it. It was like I would degrade my mission to support the local artist, to keep them here and working. It sounds Pollyanna, but I really mean it."

And it showed.

Elizabeth Leach, here in 1982 in front of a Hap Tivey painting, became a leader in Portland's contemporary art scene. (Richard Gruetter photo courtesy of Elizabeth Leach)

"She made a career for at least 400 artists who never would have had a chance," artist Lucinda Parker said in a *Portland Tribune* memoriam to Schnitzer in 2020.

Other gallery owners at the time struggled to gain a foothold.

"Arlene at the Fountain Gallery dominated everything," said Bob Kochs, who opened the Augen Gallery in 1979. He specialized in limited-edition prints by big-name artists including Pablo Picasso, Sol Lewitt, and Andy Warhol.

When Fountain closed, Schnitzer's assistant, Laura Russo, opened her own gallery. While maintaining the focus on Northwest artists, she also dropped many Schnitzer had represented.

"That kind of opened up the scene," Kochs said. "All of a sudden there were artists out there looking for new places to go."

As the artists found new homes, the galleries continued to seek ways to find new audiences. Schnitzer had cultivated businesses and well-off professionals. But a new generation was also emerging in Portland.

"You saw an influx of a lot of people from different areas of the country who had just graduated from college, who were coming out here and trying to have a professional life," Kochs recalled. "They became a lot of the younger galleries' clients, people who had become an attorney at 32, or a doctor at 32 or 34."

The next challenge was how to attract this new group. Recognizing it was a lot to ask professionals, many with young children, to visit each gallery's latest opening, several gallery owners banded together to market themselves. Drafting off a similar event in Seattle, Kochs at the Augen Gallery, William Jamison of the Jamison/Thomas Gallery, Leach, and others agreed to stay open late on the same night each month. First Thursday was born.

"That really started a phase of collegiality in the Portland art world," Leach said. "That was a really powerful moment. We published this paper and we hired people to write and it was very dynamic. We were seeing lots of collectors who wanted original art, and the prices were really good at that time. It was fun."

The inaugural First Thursday was October 2, 1986, and showcased a variety that eventually defined the Portland art world. A few examples:

The Augen Gallery displayed prints by New York artist Jim Dine, known for his pop art. Regional artists Jennifer Guske and K.C. Joyce also were featured.

Jamison/Thomas showed Ted Gordon 's folk-art style drawings of the human face and Portland favorite Tom Cramer's carved and painted wood.

The Elizabeth Leach Gallery presented sculptures by nationally known artist Mark du Suvero and Portland's Lee Kelly. Later that month visitors could see screen prints from Warhol's Cowboys and Indians series just four months before he died.

Notably, what would come to be known as First Thursday in the Pearl did not start out that way. In fact, of the two dozen galleries listed in *The Oregonian* for that first night, only three—the Blue Sky Gallery, the PDXS Gallery, and the Northwest Artists Workshop—were within today's Pearl District.

The bulk of the participating galleries, including Augen. Jamison/Thomas, and Elizabeth Leach, were downtown on or near Southwest First and Second Avenues. Over the years, galleries moved or opened in the emerging Pearl District, forging a shared identity between the neighborhood and the monthly gallery crawl.

From the outset, it seemed, people debated over how effective First Thursday was for the galleries. The hundreds of visitors making the scene seemed to prioritize social interaction over art. Street performers and vendors also blurred the intended focus.

"It was tremendously beneficial for the restaurants that were in close proximity to the galleries," Kochs said dryly. "They'd have their best night of the month."

Despite the occasional marriage proposals and less formal romantic activities, First Thursday did bring a younger audience to galleries, even if sales didn't always follow.

"First Thursday was a hit from the beginning, but it became so much bigger as it became a social event," said artist Barbara Black of the Blackfish Gallery. "Pretty soon, it might have detracted from the art itself. But people were still cool about everything, and it got people into galleries who might not have come."

Eventually, First Thursday served as much of a showing of the developing Pearl District as for art galleries. Feeling the energy of the area, enjoying the bars and restaurants, and recognizing the convenience of downtown living, visitors for a time seemed as likely to buy a condominium as a painting. But the original intent, as articulated at the time by one of its originators, carried on.

"The theory is to bring life onto the streets of downtown after dark, to throw open our galleries to new faces," Jamison said soon after First Thursday began. "Of course, most of them aren't going to do any buying. That's not the point. First they have to see the art. Then they can grow to like the art. Only then can they start coming back."

Over the years, imitators emerged throughout the city, including Second Thursday on North Mississippi, Third Thursday in the Kenton neighborhood, and Last Thursday on Northeast Alberta.

Art was at home in Portland.

······ 7 ······

Success From the Ground Up

JIM RISWOLD WAS LYING UNDER his desk.

It was 1984 and Riswold, hired a few months earlier at a small Portland advertising agency, was homesick for Seattle. Dan Wieden, co-founder of Wieden+Kennedy, walked in and saw the first copywriter he ever hired flat on his back on the floor.

"What the fuck are you doing?" Wieden asked.

"I'm gonna go home," Riswold said. He didn't mean to his Portland residence.

"No. Get up," Wieden said. "Start writing. Writing solves everything."

It worked for Wieden. The son of advertising ex-ecutive Duke Wieden, he was more interested in cre-ating great literature than jingles. But marriage and becoming a father before he earned his degree at

University of Oregon pushed him toward jobs that offered a stable income.

He spent five less-than-enthusiastic years writing marketing copy at Georgia-Pacific Corp. before being let go. He joined Portland's largest ad agency, McCann-Erickson, where he was teamed with art director David Kennedy. The duo left in 1980 to join the Cain agency, where they worked on the Nike account, a relationship they maintained when they decided to start their own agency in 1982.

From the start, they wanted a different kind of agency, uninterested in traditional advertising approaches and uncompromising in its support for original ideas. With all W+K accomplished over the next 40 years, Riswold still chuckles over his near-decision to quit. "Glad I didn't," he said. It changed his life, and, arguably, the fortunes of Wieden+Kennedy and Nike.

Riswold had spent seven years at the University of Washington, earning degrees in Philosophy, History, and Communications. While working at a small ad agency, he attended an industry awards show in Seattle, where he saw Wieden repeatedly giving acceptance speeches.

"At the end, Dan said, 'By the way, we're looking for a writer,'" Riswold recalled.

Riswold also was working part time for the Seattle SuperSonics NBA team. After his interview, he sent a 20-foot banner to the W+K office meant to show his willingness to change allegiances. The banner said, "Go Blazers."

He was hired and his first big splash would come in 1985 for Honda Scooters, starting a wave of genre-breaking TV work for the agency. Standing out against several Los Angeles-based agencies to win the work, W+K was considered "the darkest of horses," the client would later say in an interview.

Which is why the stakes were high for W+K's first big TV commercial. The agency had been generating print ads for Nike about running, but for larger campaigns that included television, the brand employed Chiat/Day in Los Angeles.

For Honda, W+K would show how different its work could be. The first spot featured punk rock icon Lou Reed, an instrumental track of his hit "Walk on the Wild Side" and a series of busy street scenes on New York's Lower East Side.

"The idea was that scooters aren't for everybody and Lou isn't for everybody," said Riswold, who had never even been to New York. "It was to make the commercial look like Lou Reed did it. Make it look like a mess."

But the attempt to give the film footage an extra grainy effect through camera exposure tricks went too far. It was more than a mess.

"It's fucked up," film editor Larry Bridges told Wieden. "We just have to embrace it."

The resulting scenes were dark, grainy, and random. Quick pans and the inclusion of the occasional film leader in the edit added to the experimental feel. The Honda scooter and Reed didn't appear until the final scene, with the singer leaning against the product, saying, "Hey, don't settle for walking."

Riswold said the final edit "enhanced the idea well beyond our wildest dreams." Experts described the spot as having a French New Wave feel. Its irony and irreverence prompted the *New York Times* to call it "the first post-modern ad."

"That just blew my mind," said Bill Foster, head of Portland's Northwest Film Center at the time. "It was so different, and it was so fresh. Getting corporate guys to go for Lou Reed? I mean, come on."

Noted individualists in subsequent spots included Miles Davis, Grace Jones, rebellious Chicago Bears quarterback Jim McMahon, and even new wave band Devo. And while the country didn't exactly come to resemble 1960s London with its scooter-riding mods, the commercials did catch the attention of a local sneaker company.

Chiat/Day had produced Nike's entertaining "I Love L.A." spot for the 1984 Summer Olympics in Los Angeles, modifying Randy Newman's music video by inserting scenes of Nike athletes throughout the host city. The L.A.-based agency also did the first Michael Jordan spot. But after the Honda campaign hit the airwaves, Nike awarded all of its work to Wieden+Kennedy, bringing full commitment to a marriage that, aside from occasional trial separations, has lasted decades.

Together, Wieden+Kennedy and Nike would become synonymous for original, inspirational and, at times, hilarious commercials. The agency constantly pushed for new ways to express the brand, and the client was willing to break all the rules of traditional advertising.

"You know, we just had this amazing synergy," Riswold said "It was just like, 'Go for it.' Just do it really does describe that culture. And Dan and David always said we were built on that model."

And another thing...

The story of Wieden+Kennedy and Nike begins with Phil Knight introducing himself to Dan Wieden and David Kennedy by saying "I'm Phil Knight, and I hate advertising."

In 1976, Knight shared the same sentiment with John Brown, a Seattle-based copywriter and the head of Nike's first advertising agency. Knight promised Brown work to support Nike's running shoe dealers, but not much more. There was one month when Nike didn't have a new shoe to advertise, so Brown's agency was instructed to create an ad "that just pats runners on the back, a feel good thing."

The result was Nike's first brand ad, an unheard-of approach when most advertising showed a product and touted its benefits. Featuring a lone runner on an isolated tree-lined road, the ad was headlined "There Is No Finish Line." A block of copy spoke to serious runners, touting "a new kind of mystical experience that propels you into an elevated sense of consciousness."

Reportedly, more than 100,000 letters from runners poured into Nike, many requesting a wall poster of the ad for themselves.

"The massive response taught Phil Knight about the power of brand advertising," Brown wrote in 2011. "It created the *idea of Nike as compared to another shoe from Nike. It was the spark of ignition that blasted the brand skyward."*

A decade later, Wieden+Kennedy included the phrase "there is no finish line" in Nike's second-ever Super Bowl commercial. In it a lone runner glides through the streets, as highlights of star athletes including Steve Prefontaine, Michael Jordan, John McEnroe, and others are projected onto buildings. The spot was titled, appropriately enough, "Nike Heritage."

8

A Stage for Authors

IT WAS ONE OF THOSE events that bring people together. It was the fall of 1985 and thousands of Portlanders stood staring at the 35-foot Portlandia statue being unveiled at the Portland Building on Southwest 5th Avenue and Main Street. At the same time, one member of the crowd stood out. Wearing his customary white suit, author Tom Wolfe watched intently as the dedication ceremony proceeded.

"The interesting thing was everybody kept (gasping) and then turning around and pointing to him and then turning back," said Sherry Prowda, who was with the novelist. "Everybody was aware Tom Wolfe was there."

Wolfe's lengthy account of Portlandia's unveiling would appear in *Newsweek* some eight months later, but the fact that he was in town to witness the event was pure coincidence. Later that day, the author of *The Electric Kool-Aid Acid Test* and *The Right Stuff* would kick off the second season of the Portland Arts & Lectures series.

The series was started a year earlier by Karen Frank, who patterned it after a similar project started in San Francisco in 1980. But after a successful first season, which included Calvin Trillin and Norman Mailer, Frank called Prowda, who she had met through a mutual connection while working at Reed College.

"She didn't have a lot of time to talk," Prowda said. "She was catching a plane. She was leaving her home and she was returning to San Francisco. She had booked a couple of people for what would have been the next season, and did I want to take it over? But she would need an answer right away. Because otherwise she needed to cancel the contracts with these people."

Prowda, with two children under the age of 4 and no experience in event organizing, said sure. She also told herself if she was going to take on the program, she "wanted to have fun doing it."

Enter Julie Mancini. Described as passionate, profane, and generous, Mancini would become known as a force in Portland's creative community for nearly 40 years before she passed away in 2022. Her community involvement included the Children's Institute, Caldera Arts, Mercy Corps Action Center, and College Possible Oregon.

To Prowda, she was a lifelong friend. The two met at a class for toddlers guided by students from a child development class Mancini taught. Prowda asked Mancini to join her at Portland Arts & Lectures.

"I'll do it for three months, then I need to go find a real job," Mancini said of her thinking at the time in a 2019 podcast.

"Julie and I started Arts & Lectures in Portland knowing almost no one, and certainly not knowing really how to manage a nonprofit arts organization," Prowda said. "Somehow it worked. People were tolerant of us and supportive of us, and genuinely happy to have it."

Together, they achieved their goal of having fun while the series got off the ground. One memory featured the appearance by Fran Lebowitz, known for her humor, as well as her brusque manner. Prowda wrote the introduction, quoting the featured speaker a couple of times, and Mancini delivered it onstage.

"Lebowitz was backstage listening to it, and was furious," Prowda laughed. "She said, 'She's using all my best lines. What am I going to say when I go out there?'"

Portland Art & Lectures was a hit from the start. The 1985-86 series, with Wolfe, Lebowitz, Susan Sontag, Maya Angelou, and John Kenneth Galbraith, sold out in two weeks. Two years later, the series moved from the 800-seat First Congregational Church to the 2,700-seat Arlene Schnitzer Concert Hall.

By then Prowda had moved to Seattle and continued to navigate her role, often meeting Mancini in the midpoint of Centralia, which they dubbed the "Arts & Lectures World Capital." She soon tapped out of her Portland responsibilities and started Seattle Arts & Lectures, which welcomed its first speaker, John Updike, on November 16, 1988. The next night, Updike opened Portland's fifth season.

Portland's series continued to flourish, often selling out in a matter of hours. Throughout the '90s, the program expanded, often featuring a dozen or more speakers each season, counting special events.

That Portland embraced the speaker series was not a surprise in a town that loved to read. After all, Powell's City of Books, a national treasure of bookstores, had been around since 1971. Rainy days perfect for curling up with a good book existed even longer than that. Enthusiastic audiences often left authors singing Portland's praises.

"I'd have to say it was the city that made Portland Arts & Lectures," Mancini said.

It didn't stop there. In 1993, Portland Arts & Lectures combined with Literary Arts, a nonprofit started to support local writers through classes as well as with its annual Oregon Book Awards. Wordstock, a multi-day festival welcoming dozens of authors, launched in 2005, and was absorbed and renamed the Portland Book Festival in 2018.

It all contributes to Portland's reputation as a literary stronghold, something the Arts & Lectures series first tapped into a generation ago.

"I'm not sure we could have had the same success in lots of other parts of the country," Prowda said. "I think, at least during the time, there was respect for creativity and ideas and an entrepreneurial spirit. (It was) 'Sure, we can do this, dammit, why not?'"

And another thing...

Author Tom Wolfe's observations of a major public happening in Portland in 1985 are worth revisiting. A leading figure in the New Journalism style of writing that took hold in the 1960s and '70s, Wolfe documented the arrival of the Portlandia statue, the country's largest sculpture made of hammered copper besides the Statue of Liberty.

Writing in the July 14, 1986 issue of Newsweek, Wolfe drew comparisons with Portlandia and Lady Liberty on the occasion of the latter's rededication in New York. Describing Portlandia's arrival on a barge on the Willamette, he called out the "tugboats, patrol boats, fire boats, yachts, sloops, schooners, skiffs, dinghies, ketches, yawls, dories, gigs, kayaks and canoes," that sailed to meet her.

"Two days later thousands gathered for the dedication ceremony, despite cold winds that swept in from the sea. The mayor, Bud Clark, cried 'Whoop-whoop!' The statue's sculptor, Raymond Kaskey, was lifted up in a cherry picker to the brow of the goddess, whose name was Portlandia, for the christening. A roar of emotion went through the crowd. I was part of that crowd nine months ago on Fifth Avenue in Portland, Ore. I was freezing in the wind. Nobody else was. The citizens of Portland were cooking with enthusiasm for their leviathan in copper, Portlandia."

Wolfe also captured Portland's unique ability to get things done in 1985. Portlandia emerged "through an exercise of limited democracy," as the city sought public input for the sculpture destined for the front of the Michael Graves-designed government building. Much like Pioneer Courthouse Square a few years earlier, a design competition was called, netting 200 entries. Five artists were selected to submit models, which sat on display in the building's lobby. A citizen panel that included art experts chose Portlandia.

"What is odd is that this clearly sure-fire and relatively inexpensive way of uplifting the public spirit has been attempted so seldom since the Second World War," Wolfe wrote. "Over the past 40 years, Portlandia stands virtually alone."

9

Brands and Bands Come Together

WHAT DO YOU GET WHEN you team the Fab Four with a Portland-based girl group?

"Revolution."

Or, to put it another way, one of the most iconic commercials in Nike's history and a game-changer in the advertising industry.

By 1987, Wieden+Kennedy was the leading ad agency in Portland, with annual billings of $35 million. Not bad for a firm that Dan Wieden and David Kennedy started five years earlier with a card table and a borrowed typewriter in the basement of a Portland labor union hall.

While W+K had hit its stride, Nike was out of breath. Revenues had more than tripled from 1980 to 1985, but Reebok had moved into the No. 1 spot in the United States on the strength of a new category: aerobics. Struggling to get back on track, Nike had the first mass layoffs in its history, jettisoning more than 10 percent of the workforce. And after exceeding $1 billion in revenues for the first time in 1986, Nike saw sales drop nearly 20 percent in '87.

Nike's cloudy outlook cleared with the help of a new design that allowed customers to see the company's most heralded technology. Nike Air cushioning had been used in shoes since 1979, but when designer Tinker Hatfield opened the side walls of the heel to expose the urethane bags to view, the effect was, well, revolutionary.

The upcoming Air Max shoe needed advertising support in a major way. So in an effort to produce the best idea through competition, Wieden assigned the brief to every one of his creative teams. That included the all-woman trio of writer Janet Champ and art directors Susan Hoffman and Kristi Myers Roberts.

Champ epitomized the make-it-happen era of opportunity in Portland in the 1980s. A Portland State graduate with a literature degree, she lived in Boston briefly before moving back to Portland, where she got a job as an administrative assistant in Wieden+Kennedy's finance department.

"Back then all the women who worked in any department had to spend an hour or two a day answering the phones, because they didn't want to hire a receptionist. But for some reason the men didn't. So that can come out now," Champ chuckled. "After two years, I was really intrigued by all the work that was coming out of there and what everybody was doing."

So Champ decided to write. She and a designer friend from another agency created a poster for National Meatout

Day that featured a photo of a cow and Champ's brilliant headline: You're Not The Only One Dying For A Hamburger.

When someone showed it to Wieden, he quickly offered Champ an opportunity. Long before Peggy Olsen made a similar trek from assistant to copywriter in the fictional TV series *Mad Men*, Champ was on her way. Within six months, she was trying to develop a concept for the critical campaign around what Nike called its revolutionary technology.

Struggling for an idea, Champ and Hoffman went to lunch at the nearby Dakota Café on Southwest Broadway and Oak. Hoffman noticed the photo on the wall behind Champ, who remembers their ensuing conversation:

Hoffman: What's that picture?

Champ (turning around): That's what this restaurant is named after. It's the Dakota, where John Lennon was shot.

Hoffman: Didn't the Beatles write something about a revolution?

Champ: Yeah, it's called "Revolution."

Hoffman: Well, why don't we get that?

Champ: Okay, sure. Why don't we? Can we get the Beatles?

Hoffman: I don't know. Why not?

At an agency that challenged its employees to "walk in stupid every morning," that was the right attitude. The women also wanted a look based on an ad they'd seen from directors Paula Greif and Peter Kagan, who had created MTV videos for Steve Winwood, Duran Duran, and others.

The directors had been wowed by Wieden+Kennedy's Honda Scooter commercial with Lou Reed and sent a spot they did for Barneys, a luxury clothing brand from New York. The grainy footage, shot with a $50 Nikon Super-8 camera, inspired the treatment the women presented to their bosses.

"David thought it was absolutely crazy, and Dan thought it was crazy," Champ said. "So Susan got up on top of the table. She stood on a chair and jumped on the table and started screaming, 'We want to use the Beatles. You guys are crazy. This is a great idea. It's amazing. Look at this film,' and they were like 'You're crazy' and then walked out. By that Friday, they called us in and said, 'We can't get this out of our minds. It's so weird. We don't know what it is. It's not advertising, which is perfect. And we don't like what anybody else is doing, so we're going to give it to you.'"

One of the many things that would set "Revolution" apart was the mixing of fast-cut clips of big-name sports stars such as Michael Jordan and John McEnroe with everyday athletes. Up until then, lonely runners and elite athletes dominated Nike ads. But now, anonymous swimmers, cyclists, aerobics participants, and senior walkers were part of the show. Even a toddler, the nephew of a Wieden account manager, raced across the screen. One of the all-time great product shots showing a runner's Nike Air-cushioned foot strike added to the visuals.

And of course, the Beatles' rocking tune brought it all together with the energy of a music video and a bravado that announced a new era of fitness. It was the first time a Beatles song had been used in a commercial and would open the door for popular music and advertising to co-exist respectfully.

"Revolution" made its debut on *The Cosby Show* on Thursday, March 26, 1987. Watching with his wife at home in Snohomish, Washington, Scott Bedbury was blown away. A copywriter for Cole & Weber, Bedbury had no idea that within a year, he'd be playing a key role in Nike's advertising success.

"It galvanized me," he said. "I thought Nike had completely uncovered something absolutely transformational, not just for footwear and apparel but for advertising. To have the audacity to license the Beatles' music was incredible."

The spot drew reactions, good and bad. Viewers were inspired by the energy. Others were alarmed at the usage of the Beatles' music to sell shoes.

"It crushed me. I thought that was the worst idea ever to do that," said Jeremy Wilson, a member of the Dharma Bums, a popular Portland band in the '80s and '90s. "I mean, obviously, a corporation or a company or a business can get their hands on a Beatles song and use it to sell something of theirs. But I do kind of find what they consider so mind-blowing in the marketing world is still co-opting."

George Harrison quickly blasted the spot, fearful that the group's music would be used to advertise everything from women's underwear to sausages. He wasn't the only one with interest in the Beatles to protest.

That's because while Nike had negotiated the rights to the Beatles music, paying $250,000, the rights to their original performance, which they also paid for, was in question. Apple Records in Great Britain sued EMI-Capitol, the Beatles' American record company, as well as Nike and Wieden+Kennedy. Though the lawsuit was nothing to scoff at, the free attention beyond the purchased airtime was welcomed.

Nike soon put out a print ad claiming it was being used for publicity in the ongoing battle between the two record companies. The ad redirected attention back to the intended message of the commercial, downplaying the legalities and saying, "This ad campaign is about the fitness revolution in America, and the move toward a healthier way of life."

The lawsuit was eventually settled, and a golden era of the Nike-Wieden partnership had begun. Nike had broadened its focus to a mass audience, and Wieden was emboldened to continue to push for the unusual.

"Revolution" wasn't the first commercial marrying popular music and advertising. Among the examples, Chiat/Day repurposed the video of Randy Newman's song "I Love L.A." for Nike's 1984 Summer Olympics campaign. And in 1986, Portland's Will Vinton Studios hit it big when its claymation characters grooved to Marvin Gaye's "I Heard it Through the Grapevine" on behalf of Sun-Maid Raisins. But "Revolution" was different.

"It broke the mold on what advertising could and should be, and inspired very different approaches to what ideas could be," Hoffman told *Fast Company* in 2017.

For the industry as a whole, there was no turning back. Kagan, the director, said later that one executive explained the formula: Make it just like your music video, but park my car in it.

Popular music became an essential component to advertising, even as they made strange bedfellows. Levi's used the Clash anthem, "Should I Stay or Should I Go?"

and Pepsi offered "Modern Love" by David Bowie. Burger King had a strong appetite for the approach, incorporating "I Melt with You" by Modern English, "Hungry Like the Wolf" from Duran Duran, and Robert Palmer's "Some Like it Hot," among others.

The practice benefited the artists as well. Elvis Presley's last No. 1 hit, "A Little Less Conversation," was the result of a re-mix used in a Nike soccer commercial in 2002. Two years before, Portland band The Dandy Warhols hit it big when Vodaphone paid to use "Bohemian Like You" in a major marketing campaign in Europe. The payment and resulting popularity allowed band leader Courtney Taylor-Taylor to purchase a city block in the developing Pearl District, where he would build a studio.

In the meantime, Wieden+Kennedy was establishing itself as one of the most-respected ad agencies in the country. And certainly the most daring.

"It was always Dan and David," Champ said of the agency's founders. "It was always, 'Anything's possible.' And that's it. They started the agency with that thought."

In the athletic wear wars, Reebok tried to fight back, going so far as to create a print ad for its new running shoe under the headline, "The revolution is over." But Nike quickly overtook its then-rival, more than tripling sales over the next few years to eclipse $3 billion in 1991. Nike has been on top ever since.

······ 10 ······

Beer Goes to the Theater

IN 1987, THE MCMENAMIN BROTHERS were well on their way to changing what it meant to meet for a beer in Portland. It was time to really get creative.

Mike McMenamin, six years older than Brian, had owned the Produce Row Café in Southeast Portland in the 1970s and together in 1980 they opened the first McMenamins pub in Hillsboro. That turned out to be short-lived when Mike took a job as a beer distributor that included selling craft beers such as Sierra Nevada and Red Hook.

Still, the brothers saw that something was missing in Portland. The town didn't just need more taverns, where adults tossed down beers and stronger drinks. There had to be more.

"When we were kids, and our parents wanted to go out, the only place to go that was really casual to take your kids and have a beer would be a pizza parlor, because there was no pub," Brian McMenamin said.

They opened the Barley Mill Pub on Southeast Hawthorne in 1983, followed soon after by the Greenway Pub in Tigard, and the Hillsdale Pub in Southwest Portland. With the passage of the Brewpub Bill in 1985, they began making their own beer on-site. The Blue Moon on Northwest Glisan Street and 21st Avenue and the Cornelius Pass Roadhouse soon joined the roster.

Then the McMenamins took on their most unusual project to date, converting a former Swedish church at Northwest Glisan and 17th into a pub and movie theater. The Mission Theater and Pub, which also had once been a Longshoreman's meeting hall, featured cafe tables and chairs downstairs and an upstairs section with conventional theater seating.

The Mission signaled two milestones for the McMenamin brothers. It launched their long-standing practice of rescuing historic buildings and restoring them for new use; to date 20 McMenamins locations are on the National Register of Historic Places. And it was the first movie theater in Oregon to serve alcohol.

"That was Mike's idea," Brian said of the movie offerings. Their first effort was a Humphrey Bogart film festival, which went almost unnoticed by customers, but was the start of a beautiful friendship with the Oregon Liquor Control Commission.

"Basically we showed it on the wall, just to convince the OLCC that that was okay, because it was a darkened environment, which is technically not as legal as they want it,"

The Mission Theater & Pub was Oregon's first movie theater to serve alcohol.

Brian said. "But we worked around it. At that point, the OLCC had gone from working against you to working for you. They were great, really, but it took a while to get there."

With the low initial attendance, the brothers quickly shifted gears, showing second-run movies for a $1 admission, and offering beer and food.

The formula worked. With the success of the Mission, the McMenamins took on another decaying building. Built in 1927, the Bagdad Theater had been one of Portland's grand theaters, but faced the prospect of being torn down. Instead, it got new life as a theater and pub, opening in 1991. Unlike the Mission, the Bagdad was a more traditional experience, featuring rows of theater seating with tabletops, and the concession stand/bar in the lobby. Non-moviegoers could enjoy the restaurant that looked onto the busy and colorful scene on Southeast Hawthorne Boulevard.

Part of the genius of the beer movies was the reliance on second-run films. Theater owners paid a much smaller share of admission receipts to distributors, and the offerings of beer and pizza or a burger usually brought in more money at the concession stand than popcorn and soda.

It also gave new life to other historic movie houses beyond the McMenamins chain. The Laurelhurst on East Burnside and the Hollywood Theater on Northeast Sandy, both built in the 1920s, eventually opened taps to their audience. Some, like the Mission, also book live music and other events. By 2022, McMenamins had eight movie theaters and 20 music/event venues among its 56 establishments.

With the rise of cable and at-home movie selections, most of the grand old theaters have shifted back to first-run films. Still, you'd be hard-pressed to go to a movie theater and not be able to buy a beer. Some have built an entire dining experience, offering wine and full meals delivered to your seat.

"I mean, we're taking it for granted now," Brian McMenamin said. "I think that's just a recognition of the times."

Times that began at the Mission.

······ 11 ······

An Exciting Time for Art

AT THE SAME TIME AS many of the elements that defined Portland's renaissance were gaining momentum, a major influencer on the city's creative zeitgeist was leaving the stage.

The Portland Center for the Visual Arts, which thrived from 1972 to 1987, redefined what art meant in Portland. Conceived by artists Mel Katz, Michele Russo, and Jay Backstrand, PCVA proved there were opportunities and interest beyond the walls of the institutional Portland Art Museum.

"Portland Center for the Visual Arts laid the groundwork for contemporary art in Portland," said Elizabeth Leach, who joined the PCVA board soon after opening her eponymous gallery in 1981. "They got a really important core part of the city excited about contemporary art. So when I opened and showed contemporary art, there was already a constituency."

The excitement was well earned. PCVA brought the biggest names and emerging talents in the art world to Portland, including Sol Dewitt, Donald Judd, Vito Acconci, and Roy Lichtenstein.

"Basically, the artists here said, 'You know, we see all this work in art form, but we need to see it in the flesh. So why don't we get a space and bring it here,'" said Christopher Rauschenberg, who also served on PCVA's board. His father, the eclectic Robert Rauschenberg, held a show at PCVA in 1979.

The impressive ability of PCVA and director Mary Beebe to attract name artists was exemplified by sculptor Alice Aycock's journey in 1978. She had four exhibitions that year, in New York, Amsterdam, Venice, and Portland.

Supported in large part through funds from the National Endowment for the Arts, PCVA proved to be a pioneer for other cities to emulate.

"It also provided an incredible opportunity to artists living here to see how the art world works, and to talk to these very high-level artists who would come to town and stay for a week," said Portland artist Tad Savinar. "So it was a real learning institution for us. It kind of stepped up the game."

As Katz recalled in a 2009 interview, the rules of the game were broad. PCVA welcomed appearances by composer Phillip Glass, choreographer Trisha Brown, drummer Max Roach, and saxophonist Dexter Gordon.

"Besides all of that visual arts programming, there was jazz, new music, theater, and lectures," Katz said. "Just terrific. It was an oasis."

The building at 117 Northwest 5th Avenue was just that for a time, as it housed PCVA as well as Rauschenberg's Blue Sky Gallery for photography and the Northwest Artists Workshop. All three, as well as Blackfish Gallery, which followed after Northwest Artists Workshop moved to the Pearl District, were started by the artists. It was the creative center of Portland, which the town embraced.

"People talk about Portland, that it has this DIY thing," Rauschenberg said. "But the part that people don't talk about very much is that when Judy Garland and Mickey Rooney say, 'Hey, let's put on a show,' who's going to show up for it? The Portland audiences would actually come. There was an openness on the part of the audience. There was a curiosity. I grew up in New York City, where if you said, 'Okay, we're putting on a show,' people say, 'Yeah, who cares?' whereas in Portland, people say, 'Oh, great, we'll bring our kids. Oh, that sounds good. That sounds exciting.' So I think there is some credit due to the audiences as well, that they were interested in and supportive of the various things that the artists would do in various media."

Ironically, PCVA fell victim to the rising popularity of art. As public demand increased, artists didn't have to travel as much to promote their work. At the same time, national funding for the arts was sliding. Even the nature of many PCVA attractions — installation and performances — worked against the growing trend of people buying permanent objects for walls and shelves.

One of the later shows at PCVA featured a performance of *Talk Radio*, an early look at boundary-pushing media co-created by Savinar and Eric Bogosian. It evolved into an off-Broadway play that was a finalist for the 1987 Pulitzer Prize for Drama. That led to a feature film of the same name directed by Olive Stone, released in 1988.

It was one of the many events that raised the bar for the arts in Portland. After closing in 1987, PCVA donated its archives to the Portland Art Museum. But the temporary nature of the content made preserving the shows and displays challenging, if not impossible.

"Portland Center for the Visual Arts absolutely helped to establish credibility in Portland," Leach said. "And if the museum had bought something from every one of their shows, we would have a phenomenal collection."

Instead, PCVA's legacy is in its influence on future Portland institutions, most notably the Portland Institute for Contemporary Art, which has attracted artists and audiences since 1995.

"PCVA had a great run," Rauschfield said. "I mean, if you look at the list of artists that they showed, you would say, 'Oh my God. You did all that in 15 years?'"

And it set the stage for years to come.

And another thing...

In the mid-1990s, photographer Christopher Rauschenberg had traveled the world with his camera, when he had a realization. It led to one of the more dedicated and interesting visual projects in Portland.

"The ordinary world is full of amazing, great things to look at," said the co-founder of the Blue Sky Gallery. "But as my portfolio filled up more and more with pictures from Rome and Paris and all these exotic places, I was worried that my subtext was drifting into a direction of, 'The ordinary world is ordinary if you go someplace cool.' I decided I have to do a project in Portland."

It triggered an idea best described on the project's website, Portlandgridproject.com.

"In October 1995 local photographer Christopher Rauschenberg took a pair of scissors to a standard map of Portland and cut it into 98 pieces. He then invited a group of 12 Portland photographers, using a variety of cameras, films, formats, and digital processes, to all photograph the randomly selected square each month. By 2005 they had covered every square mile of Portland and shown each other over 20,000 images."

As Rauschenberg explained, "It's to make the point of, Yeah, this is your city. Look around."

Not satisfied with one or two tours around town, the project began its fourth lap in 2022, with an evolving roster of photographers contributing to the effort to document an ever-changing city.

······ 12 ······

Chaos Strikes Gold

DAN WIEDEN LOVED CHAOS. HE embraced its link to creativity. He preached its importance to his ad agency. And he experienced it in the run-up to his greatest writing accomplishment: the Nike slogan "Just Do It."

Wieden explained his personal chaos theory on the occasion of Wieden+Kennedy's move to its new headquarters in Portland's Pearl District in 2000:

"Chaos does this amazing thing that order can't: it engages you. It gets right in your face and with freakish breath issues a challenge. It asks stuff of you order never will. And it shows you stuff, all the weird shit, that order tries to hide. Chaos is the only thing that honestly wants you to grow. The only friend who really helps you be creative. Demands that you be creative."

Demand for creative excellence was high in 1987 when the

latest Wieden+Kennedy commercial was being presented to 800 sales reps at a conference in Palm Desert. It was a reverential nod to Eugene's Hayward Field, often called the birthplace of Nike, where the company's founders and some early employees competed in track and field. With its focus on core runners, the spot was a step removed from the broad appeal of Nike's "Revolution" campaign launched earlier in the year.

"I affectionately call it one of the better examples of corporate masturbation ever," said Scott Bedbury. "Because what Nike was doing was looking at itself."

Bedbury had just been hired as Nike's director of advertising. Before his official first day, he was enlisted by Nike co-founder Phil Knight to oversee the edit of the spot. Or as Bedbury recalled, "put lipstick on it." To make the challenge even greater, Bedbury had nothing to do with the ad concept, its script, or its filming. But he was the one on stage presenting it.

"It was authentic. And it was athletic. And it was about performance. If you were someone who ran at Hayward field, you'd cry," he said. "But that's not a network TV audience."

His new boss had a similar reaction.

"Backstage I could tell Knight was not happy," Bedbury said. "I can't remember what his first words were, but it was kind of like, you know, we have a problem. And I agreed with him."

Bedbury, on a very uncomfortable Day 11 of his Nike career, asked Knight for a suggestion on what to do next.

"He said, 'That, Mr. Bedbury, is what I hired you to do.' And he walked away."

With Wieden+Kennedy leaders present and anxious for a reaction, Bedbury killed "Hayward Field."

Let the chaos begin.

The next night, Bedbury was on a cross-country flight to an unrelated Nike commercial shoot in Philadelphia. During the red-eye flight, Bedbury penned a new directive to the agency:

"Nike is about to become a significant network television advertiser. We will spend nearly three times what we spent on the 'Revolution' campaign in the fall of 1988. This is a turning point for a company that not long ago spoke to its customers at track meets from the tailgate of a station wagon. This just cannot be a narrow look back at where we have been. We should be proud of our heritage, but we must also realize that the appeal of 'Hayward Field' is narrow and potentially alienating to those who are not great athletes. We need to grow this brand beyond its purest core. We have to stop talking just to ourselves. It's time to widen the access point. We need to capture a more complete spectrum of the rewards of sports and fitness. We achieved this with 'Revolution.' Now we need to take the next step."

After Wieden put all of the agency's creative talent to work on the hurry-up project, they came up with a series of unrelated ideas featuring everyday athletes being active. One was even written and eventually shot from the perspective of a dog going on a walk, complete with multiple fire hydrants to examine.

With the disparate scripts assembled, Wieden sensed the need to tie it all together. Normally loathe to use taglines, he persisted, eventually coming up with "Just Do It."

For years, Nike employees were told that the phrase was a compliment to Nike's culture of taking action, as in, "You Nike guys, you just do it." But the actual inspiration came from something that was better left unsaid for years.

Wieden set the record straight in the documentary *Art & Copy* in 2009. He recalled the story of Gary Gilmore, a lifelong criminal who had spent multiple stints in various correctional facilities in Oregon and beyond. After moving to Utah, Gilmore was convicted of murder and sentenced to death. Moments before his execution, when Gilmore was asked if he had any last words, he uttered "Let's do it." More than a decade later, Wieden adapted the phrase and "Just Do It" was born.

Bedbury said no bells rang and no one in the room rejoiced at what would become Nike's brand-defining call to action. But Wieden's enthusiasm for the versatility of the phrase won out.

On Sunday night August 9, 1987, the first three "Just Do It" commercials ran during *60 Minutes.* Five more would run over the next four weeks.

One of the first "Just Do It" ads featured 80-year-old Walt Stack, who ran 17 miles every morning. Filmed as he jogged bare-chested across San Francisco's Golden Gate Bridge, Stack uttered a line that encapsulated the spirit of the campaign.

"People ask me how I keep my teeth from chattering in the wintertime," he says without breaking stride. "I leave them in my locker."

Other early spots featured the first American woman to summit Mount Everest, an amateur wheelchair athlete, and a 42-year-old who won the women's division of the New York Marathon. The organic nature of ad shoots even allowed for a homeowner to make an appearance in the afore-mentioned dog spot as a concession for filming in front of her house.

The campaign and its sentiment resonated with the public immediately, going beyond a rallying cry to be active. "Just Do It" became a call of empowerment, encouraging all to take control of their own lives no matter the obstacle.

As Wieden said, "People started reading things into it, much more than sport."

Knight offered an example at Wieden's memorial in 2022. Speaking at W+K's Portland headquarters to a crowd of more than 2,000 current and former employees, clients, friends, and family, the Nike co-founder said letters about the campaign poured in immediately. Nike bound the best 2,500 letters in a book, with Knight adding that his favorite came from a woman with more than sports and fitness as a priority.

"I have lived in an abusive relationship for two decades," it read. "But after your 'Just Do It' campaign, I finally divorced that son of a bitch."

In 1999, Advertising Age ranked "Just Do It" as the second most memorable slogan of the 20th century, behind only De Beers' "A Diamond is Forever."

And another thing...

Scott Bedbury was on a red-eye flight to Philadelphia when he wrote the creative brief that would produce "Just Do It." But he needed a different kind of creative solution once he got there.

Nike's new advertising director was in a basketball gym for a commercial shoot with NBA star Charles Barkley, then with the 76ers. The intended scene had Barkley dribbling and forcing his way to the basket, banging into director Joe Pytka, who was operating a steadycam.

During a break in the action, Wieden+Kennedy film producer Bill Davenport pulled Bedbury aside to tell him there was a problem. Barkley was wearing shorts, and nothing underneath. Movement was detected and quite visible on camera.

"It was like, 'Oh, God, it'll never get past the network sensors,'" Bedbury said. When someone asked Barkley if he had a jockstrap, he said he relied on Nike to supply him with everything to wear.

Time to get creative.

"I looked at the end of the gym at a little tiny window with screen mesh and I see about six faces slammed into it. It's kids from the neighborhood who somehow knew that Charles was there," Bedbury said. "I opened up the

door and I said the first one to come back with a clean triple-XL jock gets a fresh pair of Jordans. You might as well have had a starter gun go off. It took maybe a minute and a half and I see a guy with a jock in his hand like the Olympic torch, coming back to the gym. We had the jock and kept shooting."

······ 13 ······

A Festival of Beer

WHEN YOU'RE BUILDING AN IDENTITY as one of the great beer cities in the world, chances are you're going to tap a few kegs. Nowhere was that done more frequently or in more abundance than every summer at the Oregon Brewers Festival along Portland's waterfront.

Much like the gallery owners who banded together to start First Thursday in 1986, three of Portland's original brewers organized the festival. Portland Brewing, Widmer, and Bridgeport all set out to draw attention to the city's young craft beer scene.

"I had traveled to Oktoberfest and knew what a big beer party was like," Art Larrance, co-founder of Portland Brewing and the longtime festival director, told *The Oregonian* in 1998. "I wanted to create that atmosphere and expose the public to the variety of good microbrews."

After sharing the stage in 1987 with the Rose City Blues Festival, predecessor to the Waterfront Blues Festival, the brewers were on their own in '88. With a permit to Tom McCall Waterfront Park, they put up a tent to guard from the sun, and invited other small brewers to join in. The Oregon Brewers Festival was born.

In the run-up to the two-day event, *The Oregonian* listed 24 breweries expected to attend from as far as Minnesota, Alaska, and Calgary. Stories explained various styles of beer such as lagers, ales, stouts and porters. Subsequent accounts say 13 brewers with 16 beers showed up to serve what organizers expected would be 5,000 people. Fifteen thousand attended.

"I remember going to my distributor to ask if we could borrow some refrigerated trailers and he said, 'Well, what do you need that for? You're only going to sell about 20 kegs of beer,'" Karl Ockert, brewmaster at Bridgeport, recalled. "So the lines formed and went around the block and never stopped and we sold like 250 kegs of beer. Rob Widmer and I were in the trailers all day long, changing kegs as fast as we could. And then we were trying to find more beer because we were way low. So we drained out our cooler, shorted our orders. The Widmers did the same, and the McMenamins brought over beer. We just took it from anywhere we could find it. It was nuts."

And they never looked back.

Every July, thousands of beer drinkers came to Waterfront Park, spending as little as $1 for a taste, and up to $4 for a full beer. Entry was free and children were welcome. Demonstration displays, food vendors, and bands joined.

Beer drinkers wait for their taste at the Oregon Brewers Festival.

In a city built along a river, it was one of the few opportunities in Portland to enjoy a cold one while gazing at the Willamette.

By 1990, the festival added a third day and welcomed 40 breweries. In 1994, a second tent was added. Eventually, the festival featured an international tent, a specialty tent, and showcased the Collaborator series, in which home brewers produced their batch at Widmer Brothers' facility.

At its peak, the Oregon Brewers Festival expanded to five days and offered close to 100 beers. Parades snaked through town; the mayor helped tap the ceremonial first keg. The Oregon beer scene grew to the point that out-of-state breweries were no longer included and the festival was acknowledged as the largest outdoor beer festival on the continent.

"The beer festival really helped boost (credibility) in the town and within the state, and, to a certain extent, pushed us as a brewing group nationally," Ockert said. "We got a lot of attention because we had a hundred-something-thousand people coming. It was great. And it was just a pure festival. No medals or glamour contests."

Ockert was making a reference to Denver's Great American Beer Festival. Starting around the same time as Portland's, Denver's event takes place indoors, charges admission, and includes judging and awards in multiple categories.

Instead, Portland's was more of a get-together. In true Portland fashion, there was no judging. The only competition was getting to the front of a given line. Certainly, with the massive crowds and the beer flowing, weekends could feel like a fraternity party. But all in all, it was a testament to the growth of the local beer scene, and a celebratory weekend.

"What it says is, 'We're celebrating craft brewing, come out and enjoy,'" Tom Dalldorf, publisher of Celebrator Beer News, told *The Oregonian* in 2000. "And that fits perfectly with Portland's reputation as Munich on the Willamette because this is Oktoberfest -- it's not just fitting that one of the great beer cities of the world has one of the biggest and best beer festivals, it's required."

The Oregon Brewers Festival, like the entire Oregon brewing industry, peaked in the mid-2010s. Covid forced cancellations, and events have struggled to re-establish themselves. After a one-year return, the Brewfest announced its cancellation in 2023, only to find new life as part of the Rose Festival in early June. One way or another, the beer has continued to flow.

"We never wanted it to be a beer party," Larrance said. "We wanted it to be a social event with beer, a gathering of people with the same interest — good beer."

14

Pearl I: A Land of Opportunity

A WELL-KNOWN SAYING BEGINS, "SUCCESS has a million fathers…" Al Solheim, often called "the father of the Pearl District," insists it's true.

Start with John Gray, Solheim's partner in the early development of what was then called the Northwest Industrial Triangle. Together they transformed a seven-story warehouse on Northwest Irving Street and 13th Avenue into the Irving Street Lofts, offered first as rental apartments before converting to condominium ownership. More significantly, the late-1980s project began a trend of adaptive re-use of the warehouse district's historic buildings into residential, retail, and office space.

Or consider Tad Savinar. A decade before and just two blocks away, he rented 3,000 square feet of space on the fourth floor of another warehouse for $100 a month and created a live-work space for his artist studio. Savinar became a poster child in the romanticization of the area as a haven for artists and creatives.

Include the members of a Regional-Urban Design Assistance Team (R/UDAT) that created the 1983 report "Last Place in the Downtown Plan," which called out the potential of and made recommendations for what would become the Pearl District.

If you want to go back even further, the success of the Pearl is owed in part to Francis Pettygrove and Asa Lovejoy, who commissioned the layout of downtown Portland to be in 200-foot blocks. These short blocks created more corner space that was ideal for retail and entertainment, creating a continuous flow of variety and vibrancy. And real estate value. Never mind that developer Homer Williams, whose impact on the Pearl would come later, wishes the streets had been 230 feet long "to allow for parking." Lovejoy and Pettygrove came up with their layout in the 1840s, when hitching posts were sufficient.

Local government also was essential to the neighborhood's success. Working with developers, the Portland Development Commission engaged in a public-private partnership that became a sought-after example for cities around the world.

"The Pearl District was a golden opportunity because of its location," Solheim said. "Because the fact that nobody was living here, it didn't have any enormous brownfields and we had a bureaucracy and planning and development (departments) that really saw the opportunity and worked with the individuals engaged down here. Whether it was

Looking north in the undeveloped Pearl District in the early 1990s. (Photo courtesy of Debbie Thomas Real Estate)

businesses or developers, they sought engagement. And it was a time when the traditional light industrial businesses were moving out. And so it's just a convergence of all of those things. And then of course, the impact of urbanism came along, and Portland just rode that wave. It was really something."

And give credit to Thomas Augustine, a former gallery owner who coined the term "Pearl District" to a writer in 1985. A later story introduced a longtime friend of Augustine's, an Ethiopian woman named Pearl Marie Amhara, as the inspiration. The version that took hold referenced the area's rough appearance.

"Think about it," Augustine told *The Oregonian.* "These old, crusty exteriors on the buildings are like the exterior of the oyster shell."

Savinar, the artist, recalls the early days, before the building conversions and high-rises.

"I definitely felt like a settler," he said. "It was completely desolate and empty, certainly at night."

In fact, Savinar decided it would be good to have a gun. But when his father gave him a small Lady Derringer pistol, he got "no sense of security." In true artist fashion, he built a 6-foot long shotgun out of wood.

"I remember going to visit Tad's studio and looking around, there were literally tumbleweeds rolling around," gallery owner Elizabeth Leach said. "I was thinking I'm sure I'm safe here, but it was deserted."

The "Last Place in the Downtown Plan" of 1983 called out the opportunity.

"In a city with such a diverse arts community there does not seem to be a focus for non-traditional or small-scale local arts activity," said the report, created by a national team of experts in architecture and urban planning, among other disciplines. "There seems to be little knowledge of the opportunities the warehouse areas could present or advantages which could accrue from focusing 'leading edge' arts activities in a district setting."

The report, which drew on interviews with 60 public officials, developers, property owners, tenants, and representatives of artist and community organizations, went on:

"With proper planning safeguards, the Northwest Triangle could become an incubator for arts development in Portland, and provide a showcase for local talent. This would provide audiences with small-scale, grassroots events as mutually supportive activities to the national, large-

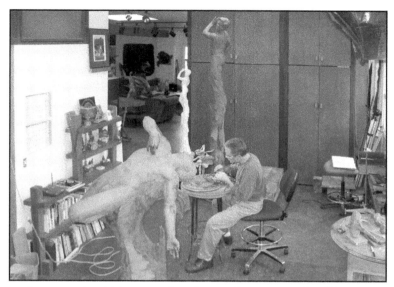

Sculptor Martin Eichinger works in his Pearl District studio. (Photo courtesy of Martin Eichinger)

scale programs offered in the city's established theaters and museums."

From the mid-1980s on, galleries including Quartersaw and Blue Sky were popping up in the area, and artists were moving in.

Martin Eichinger, a sculptor who had been working out of his house, was separating from his then-wife and found residence in a Solheim-owned building at Northwest Kearney and 13th.

"It was a building that he was going to develop and he was sitting on," Eichinger said. "I got a whole second floor in a 10,000-square-foot building, for like, $200 a month or something. It was ridiculous. There was no heat. There was water. But it was big enough for me to have roller skating parties on the inside of the place."

Solheim continued to support artists in his own way. He rented space to Christopher Rauschfield's Blue Sky Gallery at 1231 Northwest Hoyt Street, where the rent never exceeded $1,000 in 20 years.

"He doesn't show up on our books as our biggest donor, but he was our biggest donor for all the rent that he didn't charge us," Rauschfield said.

Solheim became such a part of the art community that he served on the boards of the Pacific Northwest College of Art (PNCA) and the Portland Institute of Contemporary Art (PICA).

"If he believed in your idea, he would put his shoulder to the wheel to help make it happen. It was his way of being a philanthropist," PICA founder Kristy Edmunds said. "And it was smart because we would do a project in a warehouse and we would attract a pretty significant audience for a period of time for a performance or an independent artists project. Or somebody could set up their studio there for some amount of time, because they had grant money for a year or whatever. Then soon after you would notice the building had been leased. So he was smart, but it was truly generous."

Former industrial buildings were rezoned to allow residential use, and much of Northwest 13th Avenue was designated as a historic zone, offering tax breaks that were passed on to home buyers. Over time the opportunities attracted more developers.

"Part of the way the Pearl District happened is it all was influenced by say five or six local developers who came out at a little bit different times, from a little bit different directions, with a little bit different concepts," Solheim said. "We didn't compete. We all had offices down here, came down and interacted, walked the streets, got to know the neighborhood association. They weren't sitting in an 80-story building in Chicago, trying to develop. That was part of the magic of it."

It helped that the developers were involved in planning meetings, working with neighborhood groups, and engaging in ongoing negotiations with city government officials well into the 21st century as the Pearl continued to grow.

Eichinger, who had made frequent trips to New York for art shows, got an early idea of Solheim's vision for the neighborhood.

"He asked me what I thought about SoHo-ization of Portland," Eichinger recalled. "I said, 'I think that's brilliant. I think that the only thing that you really need to do is make sure that the artists are invested in what you're doing so that they don't move out when the rents go up. They need to have ownership if the district is really going to stay viable.'"

But like SoHo, increasing rents forced the artists to Northeast Alberta Street, the Central Eastside, Southeast Clinton Street and other less-expensive neighborhoods. Eichinger was able to purchase a building on Southeast Division and created a new studio and gallery. The Pearl moved on.

Williams, who eventually directed much of the Pearl District's northern expansion, acknowledged Solheim's place in Pearl history.

"He liked the old buildings and he understood what could be done," Williams said. "He just did a little bit here and a little bit there, and it got bigger and bigger."

Williams called Solheim "the godfather of the Pearl."

Father, godfather, patron, whatever. Solheim is reluctant to take on any titles beyond developer.

"It was a team of people," he said. "I was lucky to be at the right place at the right time and helped push stuff along."

15

It's Gotta Be the Ads

MICHAEL JORDAN'S RISE TO BASKETBALL legend can be marked in several cities. As a college freshman, he made the winning shot in the NCAA Championship game for North Carolina in New Orleans. He won the first of two NBA Slam Dunk Contests in Seattle. And he won his first of six NBA Championships in Los Angeles.

But his ascendancy as a television commercial star — and a new era of advertising for athletes — began in Portland.

As a copywriter for Wieden+Kennedy, Jim Riswold helped launch the Jordan branding empire with his early commercials for Nike. Looking beyond the typical athlete-soars-through-the-air plotlines, Riswold brought more out of Jordan the person, presenting him in ways athletes had never been shown before.

So, when Jordan subsequently starred in campaigns for Coca-Cola, or McDonald's, Gatorade, or Hanes underwear, or even in *Space Jam* — a movie inspired by another of Riswold's Nike commercials — he was building on an image Riswold cultivated. And it made marketers realize that seeing athletes smile could produce as many sales as seeing them sweat.

In 1986, Riswold and W+K producer Bill Davenport were in Los Angeles editing another commercial and went to see the movie *About Last Night,* starring Demi Moore and Rob Lowe. They found the film forgettable but were gripped by a preview for *She's Gotta Have It*, a low-budget, black-and-white film by Spike Lee. In the preview, Lee's character, Mars Blackmon, was wooing a woman on the phone, with a poster of Jordan on the wall behind him.

When they returned to Portland, Riswold and Davenport saw the movie, and in it, the next three years of Jordan ads.

"The character wouldn't take off his Air Jordans when he got to (have sex with) the woman of his dreams," Riswold said. "We looked at each other and said, 'Are you thinking what I'm thinking? You'd better be thinking what I'm thinking.'"

Davenport found Lee in the New York City phone book and called.

"I introduced myself and told him I wanted to talk to him about doing a Nike ad with Michael Jordan," Davenport told Yahoo Sports in 2019. "I can't remember exactly what he said, but it was something along the lines of 'F--- you. You're bulls---ing me.' He thought this was one of his buddies pranking him. He kept saying, 'For real? For real?'"

Lee eventually agreed to direct and star in the first Spike and Mike ad, earning a reported $50,000. The spots were a slam dunk from the start, with the fast-talking, Jordan-worshipping Blackmon playing the comic foil to Jordan's straight man.

The initial ad would promote the Air Jordan 3, which was Tinker Hatfield's first effort in a legendary run of Air Jordan shoe designs. In the commercial, Blackmon stood on Jordan's shoulders and grabbed the rim, asking "Do you know how I get up for my game? Do you know, do you know, do you know? That's right, Air Jordan, Air Jordan, Air Jordan."

When Jordan walks out from under Mars, Lee is left hanging on the rim until Jordan bursts back on the scene with a soaring slam dunk. Jordan ad-libbed the final scene, surprising Lee. Listen closely, and you'll hear Mars start to drop an F-bomb before saying "Mike man, that's cold, man," as the commercial fades.

In the second commercial, Jordan says it's easy to cover Mars Blackmon, and puts his hand over Lee's mouth.

In another, Colonel Douglas Kirkpatrick of the Air Force Academy's Department of Astronautics explains how Jordan defies gravity: "Michael has overcome the acceleration of gravity by the application of his muscle power in the vertical plane, thus producing a low-altitude orbit." Spike and Mike even riff on that in a subsequent stay-in-school commercial, with Jordan repeating the technical explanation of his leaping ability and saying he learned it in school.

"At the time, Nike really didn't use humor," Riswold said. "Then we added this little quirk and I think that was the first step to Nike being popular culture."

The commercials were an immediate hit. Fans saw Jordan the fierce competitor during his games, but got to see a fun-loving guy in the commercials. It's an approach that redefined athlete commercials. In fact, you could draw a line from Spike and Mike to the today's comedic turns of Peyton Manning, Steph Curry, and all those stars of ESPN's "This is SportsCenter" ads.

With key appearances in *She's Gotta Have It,* and 1989's *Do The Right Thing*, Air Jordans became more than shoes. They were status symbols, tightening the connection between sneakers and hip-hop culture.

In 2016, the Sole Collector website named the 1990 installment of the campaign as the best W+K and Nike commercial of all time. In it, Mars insists "It's gotta be the shoes," that made Michael the best player in the universe. What's forgotten is that Jordan repeatedly took a non-sales position, saying "No Mars." Of course, the spot ended with a Riswold-penned disclaimer: "Mr. Jordan's opinions do not necessarily reflect those of Nike, Inc."

Opinions weren't limited to the screen.

"Every year after that we had to fight like cats and dogs to keep it alive," Riswold said. "A lot of people thought we were diminishing Michael. No, we were humanizing him."

David Falk, Jordan's agent, agreed. "The Air Jordan thing," he said, "made all the other deals possible."

Not only did the ads dimensionalize Jordan, helping set the stage for his future endorsement haul, but they opened the door for Wieden+Kennedy to make humor a regular component of their Nike campaigns.

*Jim Riswold (right) on set with Spike Lee as Mars Blackmon.
(Photo courtesy of Jim Riswold)*

In addition to periodic appearances by Blackmon, there was Jordan playing basketball with Bugs Bunny. Basketball star David Robinson stars in Mr. Robinson's Neighborhood. Charles Barkley takes on Godzilla. Lil' Penny, a puppet voiced by Chris Rock, watches Penny Hardaway's ad and says, "I guess Spike Lee wasn't available."

The independent ad house in Portland, Oregon, was becoming better known across the country, even if other firms might try to dismiss it.

"The rest of the advertising industry would be like, 'Oh, well, anybody can do a great Nike ad.' And that's not true," Riswold said. "You know, there were times when the fighting got so bad that they would bring in another agency, and the other agency would self-destruct within a year, because it's not easy. (Nike was) very demanding. You always had to try to top yourself."

Time after time, they did, often using humor to disrupt what had been considered traditional advertising. The secret?

"If you start from a position that everything's funny," Riswold said, "you'll be fine."

16

The Power of Anti-Suggestion

IT TAKES A SPECIAL KIND of boldness for a shoe company to embark on a $9 million ad campaign that tells consumers, "Don't buy our shoes." But that's what Portland's Avia brand did in 1989.

Right around the time a Wieden+Kennedy ad for Nike showed Michael Jordan telling Mars Blackmon over and over his that Air Jordans weren't the reason he played so well, another Portland ad agency flexed its creative muscle to take an even more contrary approach.

Borders, Perrin & Norrander, the agency that made noise with its "One Tough Mother" campaign for Columbia Sportswear, competed with three larger agencies to win the Avia account. With 90 minutes to make the pitch, Bill Borders of BPN got right to it.

"This is going to be our tagline: Don't buy Avia," Borders told his prospective clients, raising eyebrows all around. "I'll show you in the next hour why we think that's the proper position for you to take."

Avia was founded a decade earlier by Jerry Stubblefield, who, like Nike co-founder Phil Knight, competed in track and field at the University of Oregon. The brand had success in the 1980s with women's walking and aerobics shoes, and counted Portland Trail Blazers star Clyde Drexler among its endorsers.

Sold to Reebok in 1987 for a reported $180 million, Avia was No. 5 in the athletic footwear market at the time. It needed a way to compete with the larger brands.

"Nike, of course, was the epitome of athletic footwear. So we really knew we had to position ourselves against the Nikes and Reeboks and much smaller brands at the time, too," Borders said. "We looked around and you could see everybody wore Nikes whether they were really athletic or not, and that was the thought: How do you position against that?"

To emphasize the point, the presentation included a large image of a physically fit, competitive athlete and another of a pudgy guy in a casual track suit.

"The point was that the athletic person is about 20 percent of the market. And the pseudo athlete is about 80 percent," Borders said. "So we said what we really want to do is just talk to the 20 percent. But the other 80 percent are going to aspire to be in that first 20 percent."

In other words, as the campaign claimed, Avia shoes

were "For Athletic Use Only." BPN won the business, and then produced a series of winning ads.

In one commercial, a young man is playing a hand-held video game. A sweaty athlete appears on screen and says, "If this is the only basketball you want to play, Avia doesn't want you buying their shoes."

In another, a man switches TV channels to keep pace with action in a basketball and a football game. Seattle Seahawks linebacker Brian Bosworth appears and says, "If this is the only way you participate in different sports, Avia doesn't want you buying their cross-trainers."

"We're saying Avia designs shoes for active, vibrant people," Patrick Kipisz, Avia's director of advertising, told the *Los Angeles Times.* "We're not a shoe for everyone. We produce a shoe for people who take exercise and sports seriously."

The print executions were equally straightforward. One showed footprints leading from a couch to a TV to a refrigerator and back. The headline says, "If this resembles your regular walking route, don't buy our shoes." Another features an image of two cocktails and the statement, "If this is what an afternoon of mixed doubles means to you, don't buy our shoes."

Yet another print ad proved the most controversial. In it, a cigarette burns in an ashtray aside the headline, "If this is the only thing that gives your lungs a workout, don't buy our shoes." The ad copy goes on to say, "If you're not all that serious, we'd rather you wear one of those nice, trendy athletic-*looking* brands available just about

Smokers beware. These shoes aren't for you. (Image courtesy of Bill Borders)

anywhere. Because we'd hate to see all our engineering innovations get lost in a puff of smoke."

Reaction blew in faster than the reader could exhale.

The Oregonian reported that phone calls to Avia peaked at around 200 per day and ran 3 to 1 against the campaign. In the same story, Kipisz said cigarette manufacturer Phillip Morris prompted much of the reaction by urging consumers to protest, and that two-thirds of the callers admitted to not even seeing the ads.

John Banzhaf, head of the Washington, D.C.-based Action on Smoking and Health, told the *Los Angeles Times*, "It's a plus from our point of view. It's drawing attention — in a forceful way — not only to the hazards of smoking, but to the inconsistency of being an athlete and smoking at the same time."

The Mesa, Arizona-based American Smokers Alliance, a group designed to promote smokers' rights, took a different view. "We think this campaign shows poor judgment," David Brenton, chairman of the alliance, said. "We are certain that it's going to backfire in a big way."

Avia's sales jumped a reported 20 percent from the same quarter the previous year.

"Don't buy Avia," might not have had the impact of "It's gotta be the shoes," or the longevity of "Just Do It," but the campaign made national news and showed again that daring, creative work could come from more than one agency in Portland.

And for a time a friendly rivalry continued between BPN and W+K. Years earlier when Wieden+Kennedy won the Honda account, the folks from BPN got an old scooter from a junkyard and dropped it on their downtown neighbors' doorstep. When Borders, Perrin & Norrander signed on with Avia, W+K returned the favor by delivering a giant Nike shoe to BPN's office.

"It was used at track meets. It was this 20-foot thing and there was an air compressor inflating it," Borders said. "We couldn't get in the office because it was literally on the sidewalk blocking the front."

Borders, Perrin & Norrander continued to be a strong regional agency, most notably with Burgerville. Partially frustrated by failures to land national accounts, the partners eventually sold, although they left their name on the door.

Borders was the last partner to depart when he retired in 1997, leaving behind a solid legacy as a pioneer in Portland's modern advertising industry.

"They're so important to this community. They're the reason why really creative things started happening in this town," W+K co-founder Dan Wieden told *Oregon Business* in 1989. "Our industry — this whole state — owes that agency a huge debt of gratitude."

17

Pearl 2: Art's Early Adopters

LONG BEFORE CRANES REPLACED TRAINS as a prevalent sight in the area, Portland's Pearl District was a land of opportunity. And while the gold rush for developers and condo flippers would have to wait, artists and gallery owners enjoyed a shared existence that built the neighborhood's creative identity.

Along with affordability, the under-developed warehouse district offered multiple spots for emerging and unproven artists to show their work. In 1984, Victoria Frey opened PDXS, later named Quartersaw Gallery, which became known for promoting little-known Northwest artists. Next door, the Northwest Artists Workshop catered to artists looking to showcase exhibits and performances beyond traditional galleries and theaters. The Oregon School of Design also welcomed emerging talent in the area.

Still, when Blackfish Gallery was seeking its third home in eight years in 1987, the Pearl District was not the go-to neighborhood for art — yet. "All the galleries were on (Southwest) 2nd Avenue," said Barbara Black, one of Blackfish's co-founders. "I wanted to be on 2nd Avenue."

Blackfish was at 325 Northwest 6th Avenue, then at 117 Northwest 5th. The gallery was founded by art students at the suggestion of Jim Hibbard, an artist and instructor at Portland Community College.

"He said it troubled him that we get these galleries that will do experimental art, and they're collectives, but they burn out within four or five years," Black said. "Some people get disgusted, doing too much. And so we get these great galleries that are showing new and more experimental and more abstract work, but they fail. And he said is there some way we can get around that."

So the 18 founding members met at Hibbard's house every week for nearly a year, working through bylaws and policies, including a commitment from each artist to take a monthly turn sitting at the gallery. They worked together to renovate their first space, and combined the names of Black and another member artist, Julia Fish, to form the name.

Blackfish found its long-term home at 420 Northwest 9th Avenue, where it stayed for 35 years before moving around the corner in 2022. While the more-established galleries such as the Augen Gallery, Elizabeth Leach and Jamison/Thomas were in the Yamhill Arts District on and around Southwest 2nd, Blackfish landed in an ideal location.

"Within a few years, Jamison moved up here and they were all around us," Black said. "And so then we were the standard."

William Jamison was one of the best-known figures of the Portland art scene. He began selling mostly hand-crafted pieces at his Folk Craft Gallery in 1980, but with employee-turned-business partner Jeffrey Thomas, opened the Jamison/Thomas Gallery in 1985. It was a different type of gallery, embracing "outsider artists" who weren't formally trained, which fit the Portland ethos quite well.

"I think they just had a broader view of what art was, and it wasn't necessarily art school stuff," said Bob Hicks, a longtime Portland arts writer. "They just had a real good eye for the world creativity-wise."

Through his personal charisma and determination, Jamison's stamp of approval elevated otherwise little-known artists.

"If you were a young artist, or a young curator, or somebody in the creative field, and William had a belief in you, it meant everything," said Kristy Edmunds, founder of the Portland Institute for Contemporary Art. "He had this kind of impeccable taste for things that he knew would provoke a status quo, but improve the conditions of something,"

In the 1970s, Jamison lobbied successfully to allow sidewalk seating at Portland cafés. In 1986, he was a primary organizer of the First Thursday monthly art walk. All along, he was recognized as a strong advocate for art in Portland.

"Between force of personality and a good economy, he was able to somehow take it up a notch because he was a good storyteller and a good leader," said Randy Gragg, who covered art for *The Oregonian*. "Everybody looked to him."

So when Jamison moved his gallery from Southwest 1st Avenue to Northwest Glisan and 13th, he brought viability to the emerging Pearl neighborhood.

"A lot of companies came to the Pearl because they viewed it as a creative place to be," developer Al Solheim said. "The Pearl was the original creative district in Portland. Hands down. It was right here. And it just pulled people in."

When Jamison contracted AIDS in 1987, a time when such news was commonly kept private, he worked to bring awareness to the disease. He spoke openly about it, and co-founded Art/AIDS, an organization that raised money for long-term care for Oregonians living with AIDS.

He also continued to run his gallery and educate visitors about art. Black, who taught art at Mt. Hood Community College in addition to her participation at Blackfish Gallery, remembers how accepting Jamison was when she brought students to visit. He'd go to great lengths to discuss the exhibitions, even as his disease was progressing.

"The last time I went he was in a wheelchair and he said 'I wish I could talk to your students, but I can't,'" Black said. "He started to cry and then I just held his hand and cried. The students must have wondered what we were doing. But he was a fabulous person."

Jamison died in 1995 at age 49. His gallery closed a month later. In a farewell to "the great, good gallery," *The Oregonian's* Barry Johnson wrote, "William Jamison changed the way those in Portland's art scene think about art."

John Weber, the former curator at the Portland Art Museum, said at the time, "For the Portland arts community, losing him is like losing its heart, its conscience. You can't overestimate how much he did and the way he did it, the standards his gallery set, its atmosphere, just the way it looked. He was the one who kicked things up to the next level."

When the story of the Pearl District is told as part of the larger story of Portland's urban living success, its relationship to the arts is always at its roots. By 1989, according to *The Oregonian*, some 60 artists and a dozen galleries filled the area. As prominent galleries such as Jamison's moved in, it paved the way for the opportunities to follow.

In 2002, the first park opened in Portland's Pearl District. It is named Jamison Square.

⋯⋯ 18 ⋯⋯

The World Was Moving

HAVE YOU EVER HEARD SOMEONE describe a rock music concert as a life-changing experience and dismissed it as so much hyperbole? For Portlander Jim Blashfield, it kind of happened.

It was December 1, 1983, and Blashfield went to Portland's Civic Auditorium — renamed Keller Auditorium in 2000 — to see new wave pioneers Talking Heads. This was during the tour that was documented in director Jonathan Demme's film *Stop Making Sense.*

"I was one of the people down in the aisles pushing up to the stage," Blashfield said. "It was just fantastic."

When Blashfield got home and raved about the show to his partner, Melissa Marsland, it led to events that would change Blashfield's life for the better part of a decade.

Blashfield was an experienced artist. He lived briefly in San Francisco and created music posters for Bill Graham's Fillmore Auditorium during 1967's Summer of Love. His promotional flyers announcing upcoming shows for the likes of Jefferson Airplane, Grateful Dead, and Big Brother and the Holding Company bore the groovy look associated with the era.

In the 1980s, he designed the Clinton Street Quarterly, providing rich cover designs and graphics for the award-winning alternative newspaper-magazine. With its blend of politics, culture and art, the free publication welcomed work from authors Katherine Dunn and Ursula LeGuin, and artists Lucinda Parker and Christopher Rauschenberg, among many others.

But it was his work in animation that led to Blashfield's commercial breakthrough. In 1985, he completed a 10-minute animated film called *Suspicious Circumstances* filled with photocopy images cut out and manipulated with intricate detail. It was a weirdly hypnotic journey, consisting of floating plates and cups intermingled with hands and duck heads.

"I was used to my films hardly being seen at all," he said. "I made them because I liked making films."

When Marsland pursued ways to get Blashfield's work more exposure, she thought of music videos and MTV, which in a few short years had become a force in popular culture and a platform for experimental filmmakers.

"One of the things that short film has always been seeking is how do you get distribution," she said. "So suddenly, you could get national attention." That, and the memory of Blashfield's excitement over that concert he attended, gave Marsland an idea.

"Melissa sent *Suspicious Circumstances* to Talking Heads' management without telling me," Blashfield said. "And in three days, we get a call back saying David Byrne wants to talk to you about doing a video."

The band needed a video for the song, "And She Was," as group members were scattered across the country and Byrne, the songwriter and lead singer, was busy directing the film *True Stories*. His conversation with Blashfield was brief. They exchanged drawings, and quickly realized they had similar thoughts about the video.

"One of the questions with clients is, 'Okay, are they now going to tell me what they would like it to be?' But he didn't say that," Blashfield recalled. "So I said, 'You want me to go ahead and just make it?' And he said, 'Yeah, that'd be best.'"

One other detail was that the video was to launch on MTV in 28 days. That might not seem too difficult for a film-the-band performance video, but Blashfield's animation approach required dozens of images being filmed, copied, cut, and manipulated. They hired a crane to get overhead views of houses in Portland's Overlook neighborhood. A young filmmaker named Gus Van Sant, who attended the Rhode Island School of Design with the band members, was enlisted to go on the road to get footage of them in various locations.

"We called our friends who were experienced animators and others who weren't at all, but there was cutting to do and testing and things like that," Blashfield said. "We slept on the floor some nights."

Marsland, the video's producer recalled with a laugh, "We were paying the outrageously high price of seven bucks an hour."

The result was a three-and-a-half minute experience best described by the song's lyric, "The world was moving, she was floating above it and she was." There was a factory, a neighbor's yard, kites, shuttlecocks, and band members. Blashfield described his style as that of a jazz musician, with the song's lyrics providing the framework and his improvisations adding depth.

In a look back at the 40 greatest music video artists of all time in 2021, *Spin Magazine* described the video as "Jim Blashfield's wonderfully textured cut and paste." At the time, its creator couldn't even watch MTV at home.

"We didn't have cable at our house," Blashfield said.

But an entirely new audience did. Backed by critical acclaim from "And She Was," Blashfield was soon on a plane to Los Angeles for a meeting with Joni Mitchell. More followed. It's why Portlanders might have run into Mitchell at Quality Pie on Northwest 23rd Avenue going over details of the video for "Good Friends," or Paul Simon eating Macheezmo Mouse along the Waterfront, in town for the Blashfield-directed "Boy in the Bubble."

Blashfield also created the video for "I Can't Wait," the surprise hit from Portland R&B band Nu Shooz, led by the husband-and-wife team of John Smith and Valerie Day. The song, released locally in 1985, caught fire after it was remixed into a dance hit by a DJ in Amsterdam, eventually

Jim Blashfield (right) and Paul Simon take a break during filming for "The Boy in the Bubble." (Eric Edwards photo courtesy of Jim Blashfield)

reaching No. 1 on Billboard's dance club chart and No. 3 on the Billboard Hot 100.

"I started getting calls from these street-level labels in New York saying, 'Hey, what do you know about this Dutch group Nu Shooz,'" said Rick Waritz, the band's manager and the song's co-producer.

Striking fast while the song was hot, it was time to make a video. "I got the $85,000 budget approval on the phone on Friday, and we were shooting on Sunday," Waritz said.

We'll let Blashfield take it from there.

"I showed up for the shoot with my kitchen table, a lamp from the house, a coffee maker from some place, some glass slides that I thought a biologist might use, and not much on my mind," he said. "Then we had a big meeting. There was the crew and John and Valerie, and I said, 'Okay, you're probably wondering what we're going to be doing today. All right. I'll be back in 10 minutes with that information.'"

In another room. Blashfield found storyboards from previous commercials, and other props. He returned and announced the video would take place in the desert, and someone suggested they put sand on the floor. Great idea, Blashfield said. Valerie was to take the coffee pot apart, so someone got tools from his car trunk. Blashfield remembered a friend was out of town, so they liberated a doghouse from their backyard.

"So, yeah, it went very smoothly," Blashfield laughed. "And then they liked it. The record company apparently said, 'This video is very unusual.'"

You think?

"Nobody understood it," Waritz said. "Actually, that was one of the things that the band was proudest of is that nobody understood it. You know, it wasn't some girl dancing in front of a camera trying to get a guy to take her to the prom, right? It was just this weird mash-up of images."

With four videos already produced, aired and admired, Blashfield recognized the streak he was on, and embraced it to the point of sensing more would come his way.

"I hope this doesn't sound egotistical, because I'm as astonished by many of the things that happened," he said. "I remember leaving Warner Brothers Records after some meeting there. I had a rental car and I was driving away past the San Gabriel Mountains, and I looked up and I thought, 'Oh, Peter Gabriel is the one who's going to get in touch with me next.'"

Within a few days, out of the blue, Blashfield was con-
tacted about creating a video for Gabriel's song "Don't
Give Up," a haunting duet with Kate Bush that came out
in 1988. Not long after, Blashfield would take on his biggest project yet.

Throughout the 1980s, there was no bigger star than
Michael Jackson. In fact, Jackson's song, "Leave Me Alone,"
which appeared on the album *Bad,* the follow-up to *Thriller,*
addressed his suffocating fame. Blashfield was tasked with
creating the video, which would appear as a segment in
Jackson's full-length film, *Moonwalker.*

After filming Jackson in Culver City, California, it reportedly took 25 people and nine months to create the nearly
five-minute video. A total of 6,840 photographs were included to tell the story of Jackson's celebrity and the rumors
surrounding him. Images of tabloid headlines call out his
cosmetic surgery, sleeping in a hyperbaric chamber, and marrying an alien. Elizabeth Taylor sails by, Michael dances with
the bones from *The Elephant Man,* and his pet chimp accompa-
nies him as Michael flies a plane through an amusement park.
Michael also appears as a Gulliver-sized giant, restrained by
his fame. The chorus repeats "Leave me alone."

The video garnered six MTV Video Music Award nominations and a win for best special effects. It also won a Cannes
Gold Lion. On February 21, 1990, as Blashfield watched the
ceremony at his parents' home near Oregon City, it won a
Grammy Award for Best Music video.

"He's one of the top five video makers," record company
executive Jeff Ayeroff told the Associated Press in 1989. "I
deal with this stuff every day, so I know how good this guy
is. So much of what we see in videos is stupidly exploitative,

but his work is sort of a psychedelic celebration. It makes you walk away and say, "Geez, that was interesting.'"

With 1990's "Sowing the Seeds of Love" for Tears for Fears, and 1992's "Walk Through the World" for Marc Cohn, Blashfield created eight music videos in seven years, earning 17 MTV Video Music Award nominations along the way.

He also helped shine a light on Portland's rich animation culture. Will Vinton won an Oscar for the claymation short film "Closed Mondays" in 1975 and enjoyed commercial success — literally — with the California Raisins and other successful commercials. Joan Gratz, who had worked with Vinton as an animator and director, won an Oscar in 1992 for her short film *Mona Lisa Descending a Staircase*. Many of the figures building a rich portfolio on independent projects came together on Blashfield music videos.

"We got to hire all our friends on these productions, and they all needed the money," Marsland said. "We felt like we were making art, and it was getting seen. That's the unheard of part."

Blashfield took an extended vacation in 1992, a time when MTV was shifting more to reality programming and music videos were losing their prominence in the culture. He wasn't surprised when the video work dried up. He turned his attention to painting, short films, and installations.

"I appreciated it but I knew it was only going to go so far," he told *Oregon ArtsWatch*. "There's a saying: Beware of success and failure, because they're both impostors. I could see what the machine was when we were doing the videos. I was glad to be on it. But I wanted to keep my seat belt on here. I suppose I have a natural reticence. It's very Oregon. It's very Portland."

And another thing...

Not every Jim Blashfield music video made it to MTV. When one project was scuttled due to its sensitive content, it was a chance for the filmmaker to channel his inner rebel.

It was the early-1990s, during the first Gulf War, and Blashfield was working on a video for a song about the power of public involvement. He gathered a large amount of information on the cost of war, both human and financial, only to see the final product scrapped as too provocative. When navy ships took up temporary residence along Tom McCall Waterfront Park during the annual Fleet Week, Blashfield found a platform to present his statistics.

"We put them on color slides and took a generator and a slide projector up there (on the Morrison Bridge) and shined it on the side of the ships," he said.

"The sailors came out," Blashfield's partner Melissa Marsland said. "They got a hose and were trying to wash the light off the ship."

Blashfield added: "It caused police officers to come by. We asked them, 'What crime are we committing by shining light on a ship?' And they couldn't come up with anything."

Unsolicited illumination, perhaps?

······ 19 ······

Bo's Moment to Remember

IN AN ATHLETIC CAREER THAT was more about spectacular moments than longevity, Bo Jackson was a video highlight star long before YouTube existed. As a professional baseball player, he could be seen running up the outfield fence or breaking a bat over his head. In the NFL, the former Heisman Trophy winner ran away from defenses and through linebackers.

No moment shined as brightly as on July 11, 1989. Appearing in the only All-Star Game of his baseball career, Jackson was on his way to being named the game's Most Valuable Player. As he waited on deck to start the bottom of the fourth for the American League, Bo Jackson was about to become BO JACKSON.

At Portland's Buffalo Gap Saloon on Southwest Macadam, patrons filled the bar and watched the game. The crowd included a group of about 10 from Wieden+Kennedy and Nike, who knew what was coming.

"They cut to the commercial break, and this comes on," said W+K copywriter Jim Riswold. "The bar is packed and it goes silent."

What they experienced was a series of scenes showing Jackson playing various sports, a procession of big-name athletes commenting, a high-energy blues guitar, the start of one of Wieden+Kennedy's most successful campaigns, and a key driver in the success of Nike's cross-training line of shoes.

"Bo Knows" had launched.

"Everybody just stops and watches and then they start screaming, 'Play it again, play it again,'" said Riswold, who conceived the commercial. "The bar went nuts. I just thought 'I guess we've got a big hit on our hands.'"

Jeff Pearlman, author of *The Last Folk Hero: The Life and Myth of Bo Jackson*, called it "the greatest single marriage of marketing and moment in modern sports history."

"Bo Knows" got its start months earlier in another Portland bar, the original McCormick and Schmicks on Southwest 1st and Oak. Riswold and others from W+K and Nike were brainstorming for the upcoming cross-training campaign.

With Jackson secured as the campaign's lead athlete, the group tossed out associations to his nickname. There was Bo Derek, Little Bo Peep, Bo Schembechler, Bo Diddley. That last one stuck. Riswold wrote down, "You don't know Diddley," went home to bed, and woke up with a script in mind.

Next it was time to film the athlete cameos. Outfielder Kirk Gibson says, "Bo knows baseball." Quarterback Jim Everett says "Bo knows football." Michael Jordan adds, "Bo knows basketball too."

Simple enough. Others, including runner Joan Benoit Samuelson joined in. John McEnroe posed his response like a question, "Bo knows tennis?" But when one athlete, hockey player Wayne Gretzky, proved less than natural during rehearsals, a bit of improvisation led to the funniest moment of the spot.

After showing Jackson trying hockey — he was actually running on a gym floor in his socks — we jump to a scene of Gretzky skating to a stop. At Riswold's urging, Gretzky simply says, "No."

"We did one take," Riswold said, "And (director Joe) Pytka goes, 'We're done.'"

The final scene moved the commercial from sports montage to cultural touchpoint, as Jackson plays guitar with Diddley. When Jackson's 'solo' goes awry, the soundtrack screeches to a halt and the legendary blues guitarist turns critic, saying, "Bo, you don't know Diddley!"

For the commercial's launch, Bo certainly knew timing. A full-page ad in *USA Today* on the day of the All-Star Game promised that Jackson would be appearing with Jordan, Gretzky, and McEnroe that night, intimating the payoff would happen in the fourth inning, when the commercial was scheduled.

The game quickly turned into a showcase for Bo. He made a fine running catch in the top of the first, then led off the bottom of the inning against National League starting pitcher Rick Reuschel. With former President Ronald Reagan speaking with announcer Vin Scully on the NBC broadcast, Jackson blasted the second pitch he saw an estimated 450 feet to center field for a home run. Scully, recognizing the moment, tells the national audience, "Bo Jackson says hello." In the crowd, the camera captures a spectator holding a sign that says, "Bo knows what?"

Jackson drove in another run an inning later, and stole a base. After the commercial ran, Jackson led off the bottom of the fourth, and cameras showed two Nike-planted signs from the second deck, one saying "Bo knows baseball," the other, "Bo knows football." Scully said, "Bo knows 'em all, you betcha." Jackson promptly lined a single to right field.

Jackson's strikeout in his final at-bat did nothing to diminish his performance on the field, his impact for Nike, and the ideal circumstances for a major campaign launch.

"Nights like that made more than a few of us wonder if God had a Nike deal," said Scott Bedbury, Nike's director of advertising at the time.

Of course Jackson will always be associated with the "Bo Knows" campaign. But the spot also trailed Diddley, even making it into his obituaries in 2008.

As Riswold explained, "He'd always say the same thing: I still don't know what that commercial had to do with selling shoes."

But it did. With the help of the campaign, Nike's cross-training line jumped from $40 million to $400 million. It also became a pop culture phenomenon. Bo appeared on Sesame Street. ("Bo knows numbers.") Bootleg

T-shirts appeared. ("Bo knows your sister.") Sonny Bono took a star turn. Even Bo knew the value, as his autobiography would be called *Bo Knows Bo.*

When Jackson suffered a career-shortening hip injury in 1991, Wieden+Kennedy pivoted to make fun of the frenzy they had created. A 60-second commercial opened with Bo fronting a full orchestra, with background dancers in Los Angeles Raiders and Kansas City Royals uniforms singing a chorus of "Bo knows it's got the air thing." Bo knows it's gone too far, stopping the music and saying "This is ridiculous. I'm an athlete, not an actor." He climbs through the TV into a family living room and when an adoring kid compliments his shoes, Bo keeps walking and tells him, "You watch too much TV kid." After a quick montage shows Bo working on his rehabilitation, the commercial ends with boxer and grill salesman George Foreman happy to step in for Bo on stage, leading a new chorus of "George knows it's got the air thing."

The "Bo Knows" campaign continued a red-hot creative streak for Wieden+Kennedy. In just more than two years, the agency launched "Revolution," "Just Do It," "Spike and Mike," and "Bo Knows."

It all contributed to Wieden+Kennedy becoming one of the best-known agencies in the world. Not surprisingly, creatives wanted in.

"A line out the door," Riswold said of W+K's job applicants. "Everybody wanted to move to Portland."

Portland was changing. Affordability and possibility were combining to attract a broad range of creative people who would contribute greatly to the city's evolution.

Speaking to staff around the opening of their new head-quarters in 2000, Dan Wieden looked back on the early days of his agency in Portland.

"When we started, no one in their right mind wanted to come to this weird little city on the banks of the Willamette, cut off from the cultural mainstream. Hell, cut off from culture, period," he said. "The only ad people you could get to even consider moving here were people who had been fired from every legitimate and illegitimate agen-cy in the country. Or kids fresh out of school, who didn't know any better. We started as a ship of fools. And that, I firmly believe, is why we have succeeded."

And another thing...

Occasionally, Wieden+Kennedy would take a big swing for Nike, and miss badly.

There was the time the agency presented a big idea for a small revenue-producer, the Air Lava Dome hiking shoe. As ad director Scott Bedbury remembers it, W+K pitched going to Kenya to film the Samburu people, a sub-tribe of the Maasai. The connection was that the fluorescent Swoosh on the side of the shoe was similar to the natu-ral dyes the tribe created. Wouldn't it be cool to film the shoes on the feet of the Samburu?

With his small budget, Bedbury said, "Find a starving director, go get your malaria shots, and let's see how it turns out." He also insisted they find a translator for the shoot.

So the crew went a half a world away into a culture they had little familiarity with. What could go wrong?

The final edit shows tribe members in full ritual mode, complete with dancing around a campfire and women singing, the beads in their hair bouncing freely.

"It was just glorious. You can see Kilimanjaro in the background," Bedbury said. "Then you cut over to a guy sitting there lacing up his Lava Domes, and he looks right in the lens and says, 'Just Do It.'"

At least that's what they thought he said. The day after the spot aired on David Letterman's annual anniversary show, Bedbury received a call from a New York Times reporter. A linguist had called with the actual translation of the final line.

Apparently, no translator was around during the editing process and the selection of the man's last take, which seemed the most energetic. So instead of "Just Do It," the Samburu man looks at the camera and says, "I don't want these. Give me big shoes."

Not everything was a fit.

·····20·····

The Streets Have Their Names

AS THE 1980S DREW TO a close, Portland's renaissance was flourishing. Nike and Wieden+Kennedy were on top of their games and were attracting young, creative types to town. As rezoning and development drew residents to the Northwest Industrial area, art galleries were moving in to help start a vibrant new neighborhood. The beer and dining cultures were gaining momentum on their way to national notice. Even the skyline was changing, with the U.S. Bancorp Tower, known as Big Pink, and the KOIN Center Tower among the high-rises built early in the decade and the Oregon Convention Center being completed by the end.

The final days of the decade provided another reason to be proud of Portland's creative identity. On December 17, 1989, television viewers watched the first episode of what would become the longest-running scripted show in history.

It was called *The Simpsons*, and it came from the mind, and sketchbook, of Portland native Matt Groening. The series opened with a Christmas special called "Simpsons Roasting on an Open Fire," which warned viewers that this was not your typical TV nuclear family when dad Homer and son Bart gamble away the family's Christmas money at the dog track.

Over the next 30-plus years, Portlanders would get to know recurring characters with familiar-sounding names, including Ned Flanders, Mayor Quimby, Reverend Lovejoy, and more, all named after Portland streets.

"My goal was to name every character after streets in Portland," Groening told *Smithsonian Magazine* in 2012. "But we were in a hurry so I dropped that idea."

After growing up in Portland, Groening moved to Los Angeles in 1977 in search of a writing career. He wrote about his travails to friends in a self-published comic book he called *Life in Hell*.

When Groening got a non-writing job at an alternative newspaper, he sold the publisher on his cartoons, opening the door for *Life In Hell to* make its official debut in 1980. The strip was an immediate success, peaking at syndication in more than 250 newspapers.

Life in Hell also caught the eye of producer James Brooks, who engaged Groening with the thought of turning the strip into a series of animated snippets on the Fox Network's *The Tracey Ullman Show*. Not wishing to give up ownership to *Life in Hell*, Groening conceived *The Simpsons* in the lobby before a meeting with Brooks.

He had a bit of a head start, having written a novel while attending Portland's Lincoln High School with a lead character named Bart Simpson and Bart's dad, named Homer after Groening's own father. Other Simpsons family members were all named after those in Groening's family, including mother Marge and sisters Lisa and Maggie.

Homer stars as the nitwit with dubious ethics. Wife Marge is the family's reasonable center. Bart brings mischief to all he does. Lisa is the anti-Simpson—smart, directed and sensitive. And Maggie is the perennial infant, reacting to what she sees and giving hints of what she might become.

The shorts ran on *The Tracey Ullman Show* starting in April 1987 before being adapted into its half-hour format for the 1989-90 season. It was immediately a hit for Fox, becoming the network's first Top 30 ratings hit.

Groening grew up on Evergreen Terrace in Portland, the same name of the street where the Simpsons live in Springfield. In addition to Flanders, Quimby, and Lovejoy, other characters sharing Portland street names include Kearney the bully, Sideshow Bob Terwilliger, Bart's friend Millhouse Van Houten, and curmudgeonly Mr. Burns, named after Burnside Street.

The success of *The Simpsons* has been unparalleled. It its first season, it won "Outstanding Achievement in Comedy" at the Television Critics Association Awards and 10 years later, in 1999, *Time Magazine* named it the century's best television series. A full-length feature movie premiered in 2007, and the next year The Simpsons Ride took off at Universal Studios Orlando and Universal Studios Hollywood. The show has won dozens of Emmy Awards.

The Simpsons gave animated series a place in prime time. Adult-focused cartoons followed, with *Family Guy, South Park,*

A greeting from Ned Flanders welcomes visitors to the Flanders Street Crossing.

Bob's Burgers, and others owing much to the breakthrough of *The Simpsons.*

The show won a permanent place in Northwest Portland in 2021 with the dedication of Ned Flanders Crossing. The 200-foot-long pedestrian and bike bridge goes over the 405 freeway, connecting Northwest Flanders Street in the Pearl District with the Northwest blocks. On the east side of the bridge, a bronze plaque in the ground features the likeness of Homer's genial neighbor and his greeting of, "Hi-Diddly-Ho, Neighborinos!"

While the Simpsons reside in the mythical town of Springfield, named after the city just south of Eugene, Groening still calls Portland his hometown and visits often. He saw its evolution, but expressed his surprise when the TV series *Portlandia* took direct aim at what the city had become.

Discussing the series in 2012, shortly after it launched, Groening said, "If you would have told me back when I was growing up that there would be a hip comedy show based on hipster life in Portland, Oregon, I wouldn't have believed it."

Of course many would have said something similar about an animated show with Portland roots that launched nearly a quarter-century earlier.

21

Portland Hits Its Stride

IN THE LAST DECADE OF the 21st century, Portland was a more popular destination than it had ever been. In every year from 1991 through 1999, the population of the metro area grew by more than 3 percent. That might not seem like a lot, but consider that from 1981 to 2023, no single year outside of the '90s produced population growth of even 2 percent.

To put it another way, Portland's total population in the 1980s grew 12 percent, to 1.16 million. In the '90s, population increased 33 percent to 1.55 million.

Word had gotten out. For so many, Portland was a pretty good place to be.

"The '80s were fun in their own way, but it was more small town," gallery owner Elizabeth Leach said. "But in the '90s, there was this huge influx of positive people from out of town. And you could feel it. It was more urbane, more sophisticated. And things took on this hip vibe. It was fun."

Many agreed. In an unscientific poll in *The Oregonian* in 2016, almost a third of the more-than 500 respondents named the 1990s as Portland's best decade, nearly doubling the runner-up 1970s.

What was the attraction? Name it. It was affordable, certainly compared to other West Coast cities. It was livable, with bike-friendly streets, easy-to-navigate traffic, and close proximity to the coast or mountains. It was entrepreneurial, welcoming new restaurants, agency start-ups, and more.

Coffee culture was percolating, craft beer was flowing, and a passion for dining was heating up.

Stephen Gomez, a Nike apparel executive at the time, moved back to Portland in late 1989 after living in New York and then Germany for five years. He definitely noticed a change.

"There was just an energy that existed everywhere in town," he said. "That energy hadn't existed when I first moved to Portland 10 years earlier."

A creative culture permeated much of Portland, both among professionals and those who were just starting out or had projects on the side.

Shawn Levy, an author and former film critic for *The Oregonian*, described a common scenario of young people finding their way, sharing a house and paying just a few hundred dollars a month rent.

"That meant you could work 20 hours a week as a barista or a waiter or at your agency job as a graphic designer," he said. "And you had the rest of the week to work on your comic strip, on your zine, on your food cart, or whatever your creative outlet was."

In fact, Portland's creative culture became another recruiting chip for growing companies to use. Nike, with global revenues tripling to more than $5 billion in the decade, led the way.

"A lot of times we had a hard time recruiting because it was Portland. But if I could get a designer to come out and show them Portland, then they bought it," said Gordon Thompson, Nike's global creative director during the '90s. "It was a big leap for someone from New York or L.A. But once they saw that they actually could be a part of this creative community, not just at Nike, but the bigger one, it helped. Nike's creative community was very strong. But the Portland creative community was very strong as well."

Even Portland's rapid growth seemed to happen smartly. Light rail and other public transportation expanded. Mayor Vera Katz's business-friendly approach led to more downtown housing. And with more people came more customers for local businesses.

"You know, everything seemed to be working," said Gary Peck, a former apparel executive for Nike and Adidas. "There was a kind of mix between the architecture and some of the newer development that was going in. Everything was kind of compatible. It felt like a village. Not like a city."

For sure, Portland maintained its small-town feel, with an attitude that revealed little ambition to be anything else. That includes the natural rival to the north.

"I used to tell people, when you're in downtown Seattle and a guy passes you in an Armani suit, we think, 'Oh, this is some bigwig from Microsoft or Amazon or Costco or Boeing or Starbucks,'" Levy said. "If a guy in an Armani suit passes you on the street in downtown Portland, you think, 'Look at this asshole.'"

That's if you noticed the suit at all. With athletic wear companies Nike and Columbia in town, and Adidas arriving in 1993, you were more likely to look at the logo on a sweatshirt or sneakers of a passerby.

Or maybe at your Blackberry. Like just about everywhere else in the 1990s, the technology boom hit Portland. Oregon technology jobs grew more than 40 percent in the decade, with the bulk added to the Portland metro area. Intel had its most advanced technical operations in Washington County, joining stalwarts like Tektronix and Lattice Semiconductor in bolstering what would be known as Silicon Forest. Spinoffs found homes west of downtown as well.

"Portland benefited on a different scale than San Francisco, certainly," Portland venture capitalist Gerry Langeler said in a story about the dot-com boom of the 1990s. "But compared to what existed in Portland for technology business before, it was just as dramatic."

Even as Portland has felt its growing pains in the ensuing 20-plus years, much of what made the city so attractive to so many in Portland still exists. And we're not just talking about trees and trails. It's a creative spirit, protected by geography, nourished by rain, and rooted in exploration.

"I think it's always been a place where writers and artists and photographers and poets gravitate toward," said former Wieden+Kennedy copywriter Janet Champ. "I think that creative people don't tend to care about what the weather is like. It doesn't dictate happiness, or ability, or anything else. I think there's also that certain amount of independence that comes from being in the Pacific Northwest and an 'at the edge of the country' attitude. It's 'Why not, I made it this far. What can go wrong? Let's do it.'"

······ 22 ······

Zefiro Starts a Scene

IF THERE WAS AN EPICENTER to a new Portland emerging in the 1990s it stood at the corner of Northwest 21st Avenue and Glisan Street, the location of Zefiro. More than a restaurant, Zefiro was a vibe, a center of cool, and proof that Portland could have nice things.

"Zefiro really was the one that kicked the door down," said Cory Schreiber, who would open his restaurant, Wildwood, four years later.

"That was a seminal moment in the early 1990s," said former Nike executive Stephen Gomez. "We had a restaurant in Portland that *The New York Times* would write about, and people would come from sophisticated cities to experience it. And it always was a great experience."

Zefiro was where you could see actors in town on a Gus Van Sant project, or athletes being wooed by Nike. It's where ideas for future art projects, or ad campaigns, or new businesses were kicked around. And, on many Saturdays, it's where early versions of Pink Martini, led by Thomas Lauderdale, entertained well past midnight.

"It captured a lot of where Portland was at the time, just entering kind of a more craft, a more artistic and culinary awareness," said Gordon Thompson, a Nike designer and creative director. "All these worlds started exploding in Portland right at the same time and Zefiro seemed to embody the people behind all of those movements and knot them together."

As a key piece of Portland's renaissance maybe it's fitting that Zefiro was conceived in a restaurant in Florence, Italy. Bruce Carey and his partner, Chris Israel, were traveling throughout Europe for three months and, admittedly, had run out of things to discuss while they ate.

"So we just dissected every aspect of the food and the ambience," Carey said. "When we got back, I immediately got on putting a business plan together."

Carey and Israel had worked together at Zuni Café in San Francisco. While working for a Portland catering company, they met Monique Siu, who shared their interest in starting a restaurant.

"I described Portland as the land of opportunity in terms of a lot of things. But the restaurant scene in particular seemed lacking in diversity," Carey said. "I felt confident that Portland had enough sophistication to support a casual fine-dining restaurant."

With Israel acting as chef for the first time, Siu focused on desserts and finding local ingredients for the kitchen, and Carey running the front of house, Zefiro was a hit from the start.

"It was such a rocket landing in the middle of Portland that took everybody by storm," Thompson said. "We just didn't have a restaurant like that, nor did we have a vibe like that."

In naming it Restaurant of the Year in 1991, *The Oregonian* said of Zefiro, "Everything about its mood and menu signifies a turning point in local culinary aesthetics." *Willamette Week* said, simply, "This may be THE place," predicting it as a catalyst for a new, more sophisticated Portland.

"Zefiro was on the leading edge of changing the whole restaurant scene, and being part of a culture that was very dynamic and creative," said Gomez, who would share ownership in Oba and Serrato restaurants later in the decade. "It was refined and minimalist, and the aesthetic had everything to do with the space, and the service, style, and, of course, the food."

In addition to its signature Caesar salad, lifted from Zuni Café, the menu was heavily Mediterranean with influences from Italy, France, and wherever else Israel found inspiration.

Israel told *Portland Monthly* in 2016 that Zefiro was "a means of exploring other countries, a kind of armchair traveling, a global, all-inclusive meal." At the same time, Siu was committed to exploring Portland's backyard.

"In the '80s, Portland was a really traditional place, food-wise—steakhouses, pancake houses, fish houses. It made me sad that you would go somewhere for a meal and there would be canned green beans, because the thing that

From left to right, co-owners Chris Israel, Monique Siu and Bruce Carey ignited Portland's dining scene at Zefiro. (© 1991 Ben Brink / The Oregonian. All rights reserved. Used with permission.)

was exciting about Portland was it had great ingredients," Siu said in a 2019 profile. "When we opened Zefiro there was no farmers' market in Portland. That, to me, shows the change more than anything else, because now there are lots of farmers' markets and you can find anything."

At Zefiro, first you had to find a table, and Carey knew how to run the room. More than two decades after the restaurant closed, he shared his strategies as if he was planning for next Saturday.

"There were three, maybe four tables among the 23 total in the dining room that were most coveted, for different reasons," he said. "Table seven was sort of the place to be noticed the most. It was the most conspicuous table. And then 21 was the corner table where the booths met and people would get tucked in there and spend the whole night."

When he was growing up in Salem, Carey was voted the most popular student at Sprague High School. Years later, he admitted to maintaining that desire to please. At Zefiro, he would hold tables back for walk-ins, just to infuse additional energy into the room.

"When you walk in and there's actually a table for you, you're so much happier," he said. "It's like found money."

"In a way it felt exclusive because you were a part of this party every night," Thompson said. "But in another way, it was very much about the food and about the vibe. It was a very comforting place to be."

Zefiro's legacy remains not only for its many memorable nights, and for being a proving ground of what dining in Portland could be. It also inspired other breakthrough Portland restaurants.

Carey remembers Vitaly and Kimberly Paley dining at Zefiro and deciding Portland was the place to be for their new restaurant, Paley's Place, which opened on Northwest 21st in 1995. Carey and Israel started Saucebox in 1995. Siu, after a hiatus from restaurants, opened Castagna in 1999.

"There were tiny little shoebox restaurants from the early '80s where there was real cooking going on. But it wasn't until Chris and Bruce came that brought some flash and show to it," chef Gregg Higgins said of the evolving Portland scene. "Bruce was an expert at schmoozing and putting on the show."

In 2000, Carey considered moving Zefiro to the new Wieden+Kennedy building in the Pearl District but decided against it, opening Bluehour instead and saying goodbye to Zefiro.

"That was the turn of the century," he said. "I felt like I should let Zefiro define the '90s and search for something new."

And another thing...

One of the many memorable nights at Zefiro was orchestrated on behalf of Thomas Lauderdale and Pink Martini. A brilliant young singer named China Forbes was unsure if she wanted to move across country to the West Coast.

"We were all assigned the task of convincing China to move from Boston to Portland," co-owner Bruce Carey said. "I think she got wind of it, because everyone was coming up to her, genuinely like they had the original idea."

It must have helped. Forbes eventually moved to Portland and remains Pink Martini's lead singer.

23

Field of Exceeded Dreams

IN THE ANYTHING-GOES PORTLAND OF the late 20th century, creativity showed up in many places — on gallery walls, in television commercials, on restaurant tables, or in animation studios, to name a few.

Beginning in 1990, creativity blossomed on a former poor farm in nearby Troutdale. There, the canvas was an abandoned plot of land that would eventually house the nearly 75-acre McMenamins Edgefield complex. Viewed today, with its hotel, winery, restaurants, golf course, concert venue, and more, it would be easy to assume it was all part of a grand plan.

Not quite.

"That was just one of those crazy things," co-owner Brian McMenamin said of how the pub and hospitality chain's signature venue came to be.

Cheers to Mike McMenamin (left) and his brother Brian. (Photo courtesy of McMenamins)

The McMenamin brothers' collection of pubs had grown steadily to almost 20 in the 1980s. They made their own craft beer, served wine and food, and planted gardens to enhance the atmosphere where they could. As Brian said, "We were doing different things and we wanted to kind of get them all together," as well as offer lodging for the first time.

Meanwhile, the Multnomah County poor farm, opened in 1911, made into a nursing home in 1964, and abandoned in 1982, was facing demolition by the mid-'80s. The Troutdale

Historical Society fought to preserve the dilapidated buildings and the McMenamins eventually took over with an initial purchase price of $500,000.

The Oregonian described the condition of the main lodge: "For eight years it sat deteriorating and became a harbor for drug deals and satanic cults, vandals and transients. It was a depository for pigeons and a gallery for graffiti." Not exactly an enticing opportunity for lenders.

"They didn't like anything about it," Mike McMenamin said of the banks the brothers approached. "They thought the location was terrible, that the property was too run-down, a dinosaur. By doing one step at a time we convinced them of the potential."

One of the first actions was to plant a three-acre organic vineyard. The winery, brewery, and the Power Station pub and movie theater followed, along with organic gardens and the first eight rooms for lodging.

By the time the main lodge was converted into a hotel of more than 100 rooms that opened in 1993, Edgefield was well on its way to becoming "the Disneyland of bars," with multiple experiences along the way. The poor farm incinerator, delousing shed, ice house, and stable all became stops to grab a drink, and, if you wanted, take it to a picnic table or a rocking chair on a porch. Inspired by a golf trip to Scotland, the brothers decided to create two pitch-and-putt golf courses, one 20 holes and another 12, with the latter giving up space in the summer for concerts on the lawn.

With its size, Edgefield also became an enormous gallery filled with McMenamins' unique collection of paintings. Whimsical, or, if you like, hallucinogenic, what

Artist Lyle Hehn's interpretation of Edgefield. (Image courtesy of McMenamins)

the paintings lacked in realism they made up for with historic foundation.

"There was so much history in those places," Brian McMenamin said. "They just spoke to you. There are stories in all those places."

And the walls throughout Edgefield became the place to tell them. Scenes painted by more than a dozen artists referenced those who worked the poor farm, those who lived in the rest home, and even the black rabbit the new owners met when they took over the property.

More than 30 years after it opened to the public, Edgefield remains a bucolic retreat from nearby downtown Portland, a venue filled with surprises, and a testament to the vibe the brothers sought from the beginning of their professional partnership.

"You would go to Europe, and you'd see the whole family, with grandparents and the little kids, and everybody's sitting together at a table," Brian McMenamin said. "Some of them were drinking beer, some were not. There might be dogs under the table. And you kind of go, 'That's perfect.' So it was a sense of community that you get from a school or church. We wanted to duplicate that. And a lot of people thought we were nuts."

24

Nike's Kind of Town

GORDON THOMPSON HAD YET TO turn 30 years old when the young designer got the direction from Nike co-founder and CEO Phil Knight.

"Show Nike in the future."

As easy as tying your shoes, right?

The result re-imagined how Nike products were offered, how stores were designed, and how brands thought about themselves. It was called Niketown, a bold new concept that made its debut in downtown Portland in November of 1990 and would soon be included with Powell's Books and Multnomah Falls as Portland-area tourist attractions. More important, it revealed a way forward for other brands by transforming the activity of shopping from transactional to experiential.

"Nike in the future" emerged from Knight's dissatisfaction with Nike in the present, at least when it came to retail. For athletic wear, the environment often was a wall of shoes from competing brands, regardless of sport, presented by a guy in a referee's shirt.

"Retailers like Foot Locker and others, their retail environments were kind of crappy," Thompson said. "They were not really understanding merchandising, and igniting basketball or running as concepts and innovation drivers. What an athlete needs for running is different from what a tennis player needs. So how can we show that?"

As the message was slow to sink in, tensions mounted.

"There was kind of a veiled threat," Thompson said. "If you don't clean up your retail act we'll do it. And we'll do it in a big way."

The pressure went both ways. Foot Locker pushed for exclusivity around Air Jordan releases, threatening to stop carrying Nike product altogether. At an offsite meeting at the Jenkins Estate, a wooded retreat outside of Portland, Knight briefed his leadership team. Breaking into small groups, the leaders brainstormed potential solutions.

"Our thing was, screw it, let's create our own stores," said Scott Bedbury, Nike's head of advertising. "Our working title was the Hard Rock Cafe of Sports, because the Hard Rock was kind of a cool thing back then, and it would just be this shrine to sports."

The decision was made to move forward with a store in Portland, but where?

"Northwest 23rd Avenue and 21st Avenue was starting to happen and people thought we should be there,"

Thompson said. "So there was this big argument of where this thing should land."

Ultimately, Knight decided on downtown at Northwest Sixth and Salmon in the former home of I. Magnin, a high-fashion, luxury department store that had closed two years earlier after a 26-year run. Retail was ready for a change.

Thompson, whose background included designing Hollywood sets, flirted with futuristic retail settings for Nike in his designs of industry trade show booths. Long before a hookup became the popular term for a romantic meeting, it referred to shoes and apparel presented as holistic collections.

From that reference point, he came up with an idea: If Nike were a town, what would it look like? The name and the concept were the same, and Niketown was off and running with a creative approach never before seen in stores.

The town encompassed 20,000 square feet and comprised neighborhoods of individual sports, each filled with a complete product offering. Manhole covers were underfoot, sky bridges crossed overhead, and ambient sound and video played all around. Sculptures of Michael Jordan, Bo Jackson, and Andre Agassi stood out and memorabilia lived alongside merchandise. In the aqua gear section, the temperature was warmer; outdoor products hung in the cold. With a lean into the futuristic motif, merchandise was shot from the basement through clear plastic tubes to waiting customers.

The store opened on November 21, 1990 as executives made the eight-mile run from Nike's new campus in Beaverton to present Knight with the key.

"That was like a museum. It had that kind of prestige and that kind of beauty that you'd see in New York City," said Janet Champ, a copywriter for Wieden+Kennedy. "It blew away what retail could be. It was so beautiful, and so well done and so well-crafted."

Niketown Portland was a hit from the start, drawing an estimated 1 million shoppers and gawkers in its first year and being named *Money* magazine's store of the year. Stores in Chicago and Manhattan followed, and for once, West Coast cities Seattle, San Francisco, and Los Angeles waited their turn for something Portland had. Toronto, Berlin, and London were among the international outposts that opened in the coming years.

"It really put Nike in a cultural zeitgeist that was interesting," Thompson said. "We had the advertising from Wieden. We had the iconic athletes and the product that followed them, Jordan and all the others. And then we had Niketown, which was this wonderful physical expression of the brand. Before social media and all that sort of stuff, it was a place where people could experience the brand in a way that they weren't able to before."

The benefits to Nike also included direct consumer feedback that showed by grouping products from individual sports together, shoppers bought more.

"More than anything, I think Niketown changed the way every retailer bought Nike merchandise," Bedbury said. "It was transformational, because then they had to continue to replicate that revenue model and actually did a better job of presenting the product. And then we went from being just a footwear company to footwear, apparel, and accessories."

Others took notice. In an interview with *Fast Company*, Tim Kobe, a design consultant to Apple CEO Steve Jobs, recalled a white paper he wrote in the late 1990s in favor of Apple taking control of its destiny at retail.

"Nike couldn't sufficiently communicate what they were about, their values," Kobe said. "And so they started the Niketown program to sell their entire product line, but they had to do it strategically, without sacrificing the sales volume of their dealers, like Foot Locker. It made perfect sense to me that Apple needed to do something similar with flagship stores."

More than that, Niketowns helped spur new thinking about what a store could mean for a brand and its consumers. In 1998, authors Joseph Pine and James Gimore articulated as much in a story in the *Harvard Business Review* headlined, "Welcome to the Experience Economy." It read, "Commodities are fungible, goods tangible, services intangible, and experiences *memorable*."

The story cited Niketown as an example of an experience gone right, saying "Nike could probably generate as much admission-based revenue per square foot from Niketown as the Walt Disney Company does from its entertainment venues."

Mickey, make room for Michael.

When the writers expanded the story into a book, they interviewed Bedbury, who had gone on to Starbucks and helped transform the coffee house chain into a caffeinated powerhouse by elevating the experience.

"I said, 'Hey, I got this from Niketown,'" Bedbury said of the Starbucks transformation. "Niketown was like getting a PhD. If your most important customers are with you for 25, 35, 45 minutes, what are the experiences you should be giving? You know, what's the obvious and what's the not so obvious? I was lucky to be part of that."

For Thompson, the store's designer who had been tasked with showing Nike in the future, validation came at an opening reception attended by his parents. Knight and his wife were there was well.

"I remember Phil and Penny going up to my parents," he recalled. "And he says, 'Your kid ... he knows what he's doing.'"

25

It's a Foot Race

BY 1993, AFTER MORE THAN 20 years of attracting young professionals, several iconic advertising campaigns, and a game-changing retail location downtown, Nike was clearly established as a powerhouse in Portland. But it was the arrival of longtime rival Adidas that pushed the area toward its eventual place as the athletic shoe capital of the world.

Never mind that Adidas represented only one-tenth of Nike's share of the U.S. athletic footwear market at the time. When the German-born company moved its U.S. headquarters from facilities in New Jersey and South Carolina to Portland, it became another draw for creative talent, often from Nike itself.

As Nike design executive Gordon Thompson said in a 1996 interview, "I'm sure it's no secret why Adidas stuck their headquarters in Portland when it used to be back East. It wasn't because of the weather."

Indeed, it opened up more opportunities for young, athletic-minded people to come to Portland and work for a well-known sports brand. That trend continues to this day.

"You could stick a pin in that and say that's probably the demarcation of Portland as a shoe capital," said Brent James, an early Nike footwear executive who worked with Adidas. "By then everybody realized that if you want talent, here's where you're going to get it."

Besides the presence of experience and talent, Portland enjoyed relative proximity to footwear factories in Asia. Trails and open roads made it ideal for wear-testing shoes while Mount Hood and the Columbia Gorge offered conditions for apparel testing. It was also home to a man whose success at Nike gave him the leverage to make his employment at Adidas conditioned on its move to Portland.

Rob Strasser was an oversized physical presence with a personality to match. At 300 pounds and little tolerance for corporate ambiguity, he was nicknamed "Rolling Thunder."

"The first meeting I had with Rob, he threw his shoe at me," said Jim Reilly, who met Strasser at Nike and later joined him at Adidas. "I just looked at him. It was such a shock. Normally in my life if somebody threw a shoe at me, I would say something. But I was just like, 'Wow.'"

Strasser, raised in the Portland suburb of Milwaukie, was Nike's lawyer in the early 1970s before moving into marketing. His engineering of the signing of Michael Jordan in 1984 was cited as a turning point for the slumping brand, with *Willamette Week* profiling him under the headline, "The Man Who Saved Nike." In the same story, Phil Knight called him the company's MVP.

Within two years, the reality had changed, as the relationship between two strong personalities had reached its finish line. "He felt that he should no longer be taking orders from anyone, including me. Especially me," Knight wrote in his book, *Shoe Dog*. "We clashed, too many times, and he quit."

Strasser and his right-hand man at Nike, designer Peter Moore, soon began their own marketing consultancy, Sports Inc. After attempting to bring on Jordan as a client, which no doubt helped the basketball star secure better terms with Nike, Sports Inc. struck a deal with Adidas. The ensuing Adidas Equipment line, consisting of shoes and apparel, thrived. That spurred Adidas to buy Sports Inc. for $24 million and name Strasser chief executive officer of Adidas America, in Portland.

"We take the Adidas threat seriously," a Nike spokesperson told *The Oregonian*.

To be sure. The incursion of the once-dominant athletic brand from Germany fired up the troops at Nike's sprawling campus in nearby Beaverton.

"The Kool-Aid factor at Nike was much stronger than at Adidas," said Jon Katinsky, a Nike employee at the time. Soon after Jon accepted a marketing position at Nike's world headquarters, his wife, Sheri, was hired in sales at Adidas.

"From the Adidas side, everybody was fine. Nobody really ever made a big deal about it," Sheri said. "Nike on the other hand... Jon especially was very paranoid."

The couple moved to Portland from the Southeast region of the country. In addition to learning not to pump their own gas and how to sort recyclables, they had to navigate their Nike-Adidas mixed marriage.

"A lot of Nike people literally would not socialize with us as a couple because Sheri worked for Adidas," Jon said. "You've got to remember, this was a time that Adidas was aggressively expanding and aggressively recruiting and paying Nike employees to jump ship. So there was a lot of sensitivity to that. We just kind of got caught in the middle of it."

The caution was its most comical at the Portland Airport, where Nike and Adidas employees flew in and out of every day. Today, Jon and Sheri laugh at the measures they took.

"If we traveled anywhere together I had to go like five or 10 steps ahead of Jon or behind him because he had Nike bags and I had Adidas bags and we could not be seen with the commingling of each other's bag," Sheri said.

"Or I would pick her up at baggage claim, and I would give her a kiss," Jon said. "But then I would walk ahead or have her grab her bag herself because you know how small that airport is. All I needed was for Phil Knight or somebody to see me yanking Adidas bags."

No one took the perceived rivalry more seriously than Knight, who called Strasser's move to Adidas "the ultimate betrayal." In fact, when rumors flew that Adidas was putting together an elite running team for Portland's annual Hood-to-Coast Relay in 1994, Nike employee and former marathon world-record holder Alberto Salazar assembled a top team of his own. And when the Nike team narrowly won the normally collegial 200-mile run, Knight called an all-company meeting on the campus and awarded Salazar a new BMW convertible.

Adidas cracked back with a print ad showing its runners passing by a broken down BMW.

Outgunned from the start, the rivalry on the Adidas side was less intense. Strasser's tenure at Adidas was brief, as he died of a massive heart attack less than nine months after taking charge. Moore took over as the head of Adidas America, which had growing pains

"The rivalry was actually Adidas in the United States versus Germany," said Gary Peck, an apparel executive who moved from Nike to Adidas. Struggles over control from the parent organization and operational independence in the U.S. made Adidas "its own worst enemy" according to Peck.

"Nike played the game to win. Adidas played the game not to lose," he said. "It was a very different philosophical way of operating a business."

Boosted by an aggressive move into soccer in the mid-1990s, Nike outpaced Adidas globally. In Portland, the template was set, with marketers, designers, and other business experts being drawn to Nike or Adidas, or any of the other athletic wear companies then and in the future.

Names like Keen, Fila, Li Ning and, much later, Under Armour all came to Portland. Niche brands creating shoes for everything from cyclists to nurses to restaurant cooks followed, as did jobs in design production, video, marketing, and advertising. It all brought more creative talent to town.

"If someone left either Nike and or Adidas, they left because they had an idea, they were an entrepreneur who wanted to set up shop, and they weren't going to get out of Dodge, because this was their home," Peck said. "So the thing just started growing. It was no different than if you looked at the history of software in Silicon Valley."

Except with sneakers.

······ 26 ······

Pearl 3: A Place to Call Home

PORTLAND CERTAINLY DID NOT START the urban residential renaissance that swept America in the late 20th century, but it embraced it so successfully that its local epicenter, the Pearl District, became the quintessential rags-to-riches story.

Bill Foster grew up in Portland long before the neighborhood north of Burnside became filled with high-rise condominiums, restaurants, stores, and galleries. He remembers driving through the area as a teen.

"It looked hopeless," he said. "It was all empty warehouses and train spurs and giant potholes that made you wonder, 'How deep is that? Can I make it?'"

The 1990 census counted only 629 people living in the Pearl District, with nearly half making less than $10,000 a year. At the same time, the path was clear. With a handful of artists and others as early settlers, and developers beginning to create living spaces, people were ready to adopt the Pearl.

"I read an article, probably in the '90s, that said real estate follows art," said longtime Pearl District real estate broker Debbie Thomas. "I kind of took it to heart by remembering that the galleries make it not a scary area."

Not scary, but still not fully developed either. Keith Peters was an original owner in the first new residential building built in the Pearl, the Pearl Lofts at Northwest 10th and Hoyt. Built in 1994, the Pearl Lofts offered 27 loft-style condos in a three-story building.

"There were no services whatsoever," Peters said of the neighborhood. "No restaurants, except for Shakers (a café that opened in 1991 on Northwest 12th and Glisan). There were no grocery stores, no dry cleaners, that kind of thing."

Despite that, the Pearl Lofts sold out more than a year before they were finished, at prices ranging from $70,000 to $160,000. Residents like Peters were confident more would come in time.

"The sales presentation that we went to wasn't just about 10th and Hoyt, that building," he said. "Even in that first presentation, it was with the PDC's (Portland Development Commission) vision for the Pearl."

The romance of the Pearl, along with the creative identity produced by the arts and galleries, was the conversion of historic buildings. Al Solheim's Irving Street Lofts building was the first, originally offering only rental units. Farther south on historic Northwest 13th the Chown Pella Lofts would be the first former warehouse to be converted for individual ownership.

"I think there's alternatives to gobbling up farmland. The theme is increasing densities within the urban core," developer John Carroll told *Portland Business Journal* in 1995, vocalizing the intent of the urban growth boundary and plans to encourage urban living.

The Chown Pella was built in 1910 with seven stories. A year later, a four-story building was added to the north side. Carroll purchased it in 1993 and added a fifth story to the north building.

Visits to other cities including Chicago, Denver, and San Francisco helped define exactly what the Chown Pella should be. Carroll suggested most of the space should be devoted to deeded condominiums and asked Thomas what she thought.

"I said I think that would be unbelievably cool," she recalled. "It was going to shake out to be about 70 units. I said I don't know about 70, though. Would people want to live in a building with 70 other people?"

The Chown Pella would comprise 68 loft-style condominiums and six ground-floor retail spaces. Thomas was tasked with selling the units as they came ready in 1996, despite her focus on commercial deals in the area.

She recalled how Carroll reacted when she suggested he hire a residential real estate expert. "He said, 'We're telling a story about the neighborhood and that's what you know. We're not selling a house in the West Hills, so I don't want someone who does that.'"

The marketing reflected that story, touting "Industrial strength living in the Pearl District." Ads called out the 10-foot beamed ceilings, exposed brick walls, and city and

The Chown Pella Lofts is the Pearl District's first building to be converted for condominiums.

mountain views, under the headline, "Sorry, this offer isn't available in the 'burbs." A humorous guide to living in an urban dwelling included edicts that Elvis will be played whenever appropriate and pets that miss their owners during the day will get a job.

During the first six weeks, sales averaged nearly one a day as buyers flocked to the Pearl, a rush that would last for years. Units ranged from just more than 700 square feet to more than 1800.

With most of the units priced well below $200,000, the Chown Pella attracted a broad range of buyers, including singles and couples. Their professions ranged from artists and other creative pursuits, to mid-level corporate managers, to attorneys, and retirees.

"It was a real huge mixed bag because of the size of some of the units," Thomas said.

As residents came to the Pearl, so did businesses to serve them. Bima restaurant opened on Northwest 13th and Hoyt. Salons, furniture stores, and a gym opened. And of course, art galleries continued to draw visitors.

The rapid expansion would continue. Carroll built the McKenzie Lofts, which opened in 1997 at Northwest 12th and Glisan, as well as the 15-story Elizabeth Lofts, which opened in 2005 at Northwest 9th and Flanders. In addition to buyers, the Pearl attracted officials and developers from all over to talk with key players in the neighborhood's development.

"We had 100 or more different cities come into town," Thomas said. "They'd come into my office, or John Carroll's office, to ask how to do it, how to do it, how to do it."

The magic of early development in the Pearl District was its historic feel. The neighborhood around Northwest 13th looked as if it was from the early 1900s, even as the living units boasted modern interiors. In fact, when Carroll opened Mckenzie Lofts a block from the Chown Pella in 1998, the new building was designed to look like it was from an earlier era.

"Some of the biggest compliments we've received have been from people who say, 'What a great, old renovated building,'" Carroll said at the time. "We wanted to design a building that looked as if it had been part of the community."

For her part, Thomas said the transformation of the Pearl was a steady, ongoing evolution that reached an accelerated pace in the late 1990s.

"How many people really get to watch a brand new neighborhood be created and not even know it," she said. "Because I was just going to work and putting one foot in front of the next and seeing these cool, exciting things going on."

······ 27 ······

Please Welcome to the Stage

(Disclaimer: Music is subjective, as were the choices of what to include here. There were enough artists, bands, and clubs I could have included that it could be a book of its own.)

YOU KIND OF HAD TO be there.

That seems the best way to sum up Portland's music scene in the 1980s and '90s, a time when fame was fleeting, but music was everywhere. Clubs welcomed audiences for blues, jazz, and rock in all its permutations, providing a stage for legendary performers as well as passionate dreamers, ranging from jazz drummer Mel Brown, blues singer Paul deLay, punk rockers the Wipers, and early hip-hop artists the U-Krew. Annual events such as the Waterfront Blues Festival, the Cathedral Park Jazz Festival, and the Mayor's Ball opened the doors to larger audiences.

The clubs are long gone, but not forgotten. Spots like the Last Hurrah, X-Ray Café, Key Largo, Candlelight Room, Jazz de Opus, Jimmy Mak's, and countless others all helped build Portland's lasting reputation as a vibrant, eclectic music town.

The spot that might have been the city's most vibrant and eclectic was Satyricon on Northwest 6th and Davis. Audiences navigating the thriving heroin traffic in Old Town could see a wide range of musical styles as well as poetry readings and experimental performance art. Equal parts dangerous and communal, it was often called the CBGB of the West Coast after the New York punk rock-new wave mecca that launched the careers of the Ramones, Talking Heads, and Blondie, among others.

In 1987, recent high school graduate Jeremy Wilson and his band the Dharma Bums began playing at Satyricon on their way to becoming one of the most popular acts in Portland. Their post-punk, early-alternative rock was compared to R.E.M. with more force, apt when you listen to "Boots of Leather," off their first album, *Haywire,* or "Pumpkinhead" from 1990's *Bliss.*

"It was exhilarating," Wilson said of the band's rise. "There was so much energy around what we were doing. We knew that we weren't on anybody's radar or anything. But we knew we were fucking special."

So did others. In a 2010 Portland show, Jeff Tweedy, lead singer for Wilco, referred to his late-'80s material with Uncle Tupelo as a time when "there was only one band in Portland: the Dharma Bums."

Wilson grew up in Scotts Mills, a town of fewer than 300 people about 40 miles south of Portland. He excelled in ballet as a kid, which earned him merciless attacks from other kids, and led him deeply into playing guitar and writing songs. The Dharma Bums already were Wilson's third band by age 17, as the group's age was not a hindrance to Satyricon owner George Touhouliotis — with a caveat.

Wilson, mimicking Touhouliotis' heavy Greek accent, explained: "He'd say, 'Jeremy, I like your band. The girls come. It's good. You can come in here anytime you like, but I don't want you to get into the beer. And one last thing, if you see the cops come in, you go out the back door.'"

Instead, Wilson remained front and center on the Portland scene for years, overpowering the stage with his constant movement and driven performance. He became friends with members of R.E.M. and played his unproduced demos for Heatmiser's Elliott Smith, who would soon go solo and move toward a stripped-down sound of his own. Nirvana opened for the Dharma Bums at Satyricon one night in 1988, and Courtney Love has said it was the night she met Kurt Cobain.

"Kurt really, truly loved the Dharma Bums. He told me so," Wilson recalled. "For me, that's a beautiful and a wonderful memory of mine. He also once cried on my shoulder when *Nevermind* was starting to really take off."

White-hot fame eluded Portland's music stars. There were the occasional hits, such as "Harden My Heart" from Quarterflash in 1981 and "I Can't Wait" by Nu Shooz in 1985, which both reached No. 3 on the Billboard Hot 100. And Portland could take pride in hearing Smith's Oscar-nominated song "Miss Misery" in director Gus Van Sant's *Good Will Hunting* in 1997, or in club favorites the Dandy Warhols signing with major label Capitol Records that same year. But overall, Portland built a reputation as a good music town, predominantly for Portland audiences.

"There was a sense that Portland was known, but it never quite had a moment as big as, say, Athens had when B-52s and R.E.M. came up or that Seattle had with Nirvana and Soundgarden and those bands, or Minneapolis had with the Replacements and Husker Du," said longtime Portland popular music critic Marty Hughley. "You know, the Raleigh-Chapel Hill scene and a few other places, Portland kind of was on that level. So it was known, but it never had that sort of brush-fire kind of moment."

Portland bands in the 1980s and '90s never became the next big thing. Despite loyal followings, record contracts, and album releases as well as regional, national, and European tours, it just didn't happen. Some situations proved comic, others tragic.

Start with Billy Rancher and the Unreal Gods. With go-go dancers, wild outfits and makeup, the band stood out, even in weird Portland. Rancher signed a six-record deal with Arista and Clive Davis in 1983 but tensions over individual songs, personnel, and even the band's name scuttled the project. Rancher, having seemingly beat cancer once, had a recurrence and died in 1986.

Another Portland favorite, the Crazy 8s, blended rock, ska, and funk to thrive as a dance band. After incessantly heavy travel to clubs and colleges around the county, the band broke up after 12 years. Manager Marc Baker summed up the group's frustrations about their journey.

"I'll never forget the guy from MCA," Baker told *The Oregonian* in 1994. "He came up to see us at Starry Night (now the Roseland Theater at Northwest 6th and Burnside). Afterward he said, `You guys are the greatest band I've ever seen. But I'm looking for the next Tiffany.' (A teen bubble gum star at the time.) We all fell out laughing. To us, that was the whole music business in 30 seconds."

In Hughley's view, the biggest head-scratcher was funk-and-soul band Cool'r, whom he called "players' players" for their musicianship. "Over and over again, you'd just sit there and your jaw is dropping by what these guys could do," he said. The band was eventually signed to A&M records, with legendary producer Lou Adler coming out of retirement to take on the project. But their self-titled album for A&M in 1988 failed to capture their onstage magic.

The Dan Reed Network seemed on the verge of breaking big when they opened for Bon Jovi on a European Tour in 1989, but U.S. record sales for their funk-rock style were fleeting. The band also was slated to open for the Rolling Stones on their European Tour in 1990, but saw the first show at London's Wembley Stadium canceled during sound check due to what was stated as a finger injury to Stones guitarist Keith Richards. The tour eventually got underway a week later, but at the time it must have felt like just another bad break for Portland bands.

Perhaps the most tragic was the story of Smith, the former member of Heatmiser who found fame as a solo artist with his somber, anti-grunge music. He'd moved to Los Angeles and was living with his girlfriend when, as battles with depression and addiction seemed to take over his life, he died in 2003 of two stab wounds to the chest. A brief suicide note written on a post-it was found, but the coroner could not determine if the wounds were self-inflicted.

Wilson pointed to changes in the music business as a key factor in the struggle for Portland bands to make it big. Gone were the days of major studios granting artists multiple-album recording contracts and giving them time to grow as Columbia did for Bruce Springsteen in the early-'70s. In fact, the musical nuclear explosion created by Nirvana, which drew great attention to the Northwest, also reinforced record labels' belief that bands could find their audiences quickly and without nurturing.

An exception to the relative obscurity of Portland bands in the '90s was Everclear. The group's founder, Art Alexakis, moved to Portland after failing to make it in Los Angeles and San Francisco and took out a newspaper ad to find band members. The alternative rock band achieved broad success with hits like "Santa Monica," "Father of Mine," and "I Will Buy You a New Life" even as Alexakis was turning off his adopted city with his relentless quest for fame.

"I think there's a lot of places where Art Alexakis would have been the norm," Hughley said. "Here, he was really an outlier because he was so nakedly ambitious."

Therein might lie the secret of the Portland music scene in the late-20th century. A DIY culture, enthusiastic audiences, and artists performing for the love of it — and rent money — made for a unique scene that became known for its universe rather than its shooting stars.

Zia McCabe of the Dandy Warhols said as much in a 2014 interview with *Vortex Music Magazine.*

"Everybody made music for themselves — not for a trend and not to have any commercial potential," she said. "There was no commercial potential so that didn't matter! Everybody just did what they wanted" and embraced a "freedom of expression that I don't think many cities have."

But with the dawn of the 21st century, it all changed. Advances in recording technology allowed artists to make better-sounding records for a fraction of the cost, and the growth of the Internet meant music — formal recordings or live performances — could be shared far and wide.

"It becomes much more possible for everybody to make their record and get it out there, and it sounds relatively professional," Hughley said. "All of a sudden, you'll have played three gigs in your hometown, but you'll have a whole bunch of fans in New Jersey and England and whatever and that changes the dynamic entirely."

The independent scene thrived in the early 2000s in Portland, a city still affordable for musicians and increasingly known as a cool place to live. Colin Meloy moved to town from Montana and in 2000 formed the Decemberists with former Dharma Bums member John Moen on drums. In 2001, the Shins relocated to Portland from Albuquerque, New Mexico, and released the single, "New Slang," which became a huge independent hit and launched band leader James Mercer's career. Portugal. The Man came from Alaska and Modest Mouse moved in from Washington. Homegrown talents Blitzen Trapper and Grammy Award winner Esperanza Spalding gained prominence.

The Portland music scene is a long way from those days in the '80s and '90s when live music was all that mattered. It's a time worth remembering, especially to those who were there.

"Because it was communal. It was church. You know, it was energy," said Wilson, who was on a mission greater than record sales. "I thought rock and roll could change the world. That didn't mean I wanted to be famous. I mean I wanted to change the world."

And another thing...

Certainly there were plenty of bad shows in Portland in the 1980s and '90s. But not all of them got songs written about them. Such was the case for Minnesota alternative band the Replacements, notoriously talented but wreck-less rockers whose show on December 7, 1987 at the Pine Street Theater was widely regarded as their worst.

Tales of band members sharing clothes, some of which went into the audience, and an incoherent performance were just part of it. Backstage, lead singer Paul Westerberg kicked it up a notch by swinging on a chandelier and pulling it out of the ceiling. Accounts vary on whether a full-size couch went out the window before or after the show.

"I do have a memory of standing there watching the show, and yes, it was awful," said Jeremy Wilson of the Dharma Bums. "Yeah, it was embarrassing. It was horrible. I mean, the alcoholism and just sort of the irreverence of every-thing. I mean, it's one thing to hate capitalism. But it's quite another thing to hate your audience. The people are here for escape. People are here because they love you.

People are here because they connect. I can understand the Bob Dylan point of view of, 'I'm not responsible for that,' but you took their money, right?"

There must have been some regret. Westerberg soon wrote the song "Portland," although it wasn't included on a record until 1997's All for Nothing/Nothing for All compilation. Notably, as the song fades, Westerberg says, "Portland, we're sorry."

Years later, Westerberg did a free solo show at Music Millennium on Northwest 23rd Avenue. Emerging from his bus for the afternoon performance, he took his guitar to the stage and struggled with his own chords and lyrics, with those in the audience having to feed him lines.

It was very on-brand.

28

Putting Portland on the Table

LOOKING BACK, THE ABUNDANCE OF farmers, growers, fishers, and the like throughout the Northwest made Portland a prime candidate to embrace the farm-to-table movement, which emphasizes the use of locally sourced, in-season ingredients in the creation of imaginative, only-of-their-place recipes and dishes. But it took a few chefs committed to the concept for the movement to take hold and thrive in Portland in the mid-1990s.

By the time he was in his early 30s, chef Greg Higgins had helped build the restaurant at the Heathman Hotel into one of the top dining destinations in Portland. He also managed B. Moloch Heathman Bakery and Pub, which featured onsite brewing from Widmer Brothers and a menu of pizza, salads, pastas, and fresh baked goods. At the same time, he was building a network of local producers who supplied the bounty from their farms and gardens that starred in Higgins' inventive dishes.

But something was missing, or getting in the way.

"I knew that I didn't want to be a hotel chef forever," Higgins said. "It was a great vehicle for me, but after about 10 years of banquets and room service, brunch, and high tea and stuff, you start realizing that it's distracting from what you really want to do."

Higgins grew up in rural New York and spent time working on a dairy farm. His vision, similar to that of famed chef Alice Waters of Chez Panisse in Berkeley, California, was exclusively, passionately local. He cultivated and relied on ingredients from the Northwest.

"Greg understood the agriculture and the region," said restaurateur and farm-to-table advocate Cory Schreiber. "He was as deeply committed to that as anybody."

Higgins' commitment and his role at the Heathman often were in conflict.

"At a hotel, you know, if Pavarotti wants raspberries in February, you get them and he gets them," he said. "That stuff always kind of grated on me because it was against my philosophy."

Even as the Heathman was named *The Oregonian's* Restaurant of the Year in 1988, Higgins was looking to open his own restaurant. The opportunity eventually came at Southwest Broadway and Jefferson, where Paul Mallory, who tended bar at what was then the Broadway Revue Restaurant, alerted Higgins to its availability. The two finalized the purchase in January 1994. Higgins Restaurant opened two months later.

During a frenetic renovation of the space before opening, Higgins found time to write an essay that articulated exactly what he wanted his restaurant to be. It became a mission statement for Portland's earliest farm-to-table restaurant and provided a guide to like-minded chefs looking to be part of the emerging sustainable food movement.

It reads:

"There exists today a growing need for our commitment to sustainable food practices. This broad and complex topic relates to a responsibility that we all share in the stewardship of our soil, water and air.

"We believe strongly in farming techniques which are sustainable, organic and regenerative. It is imperative that we re-establish the balance between nature and man in all our food producing endeavors. Current large farming methods rely on a system of agriculture dependent on the use of herbicides, pesticides, petrochemicals and intensive irrigation. This system is non-renewable, non-sustainable and generally non-local.

"Alternatives exist in the form of small local farms practicing sound organic agricultural methods. These local farms restore the fabric of rural communities, decrease water and air pollution, preserve and build topsoil and produce superb crops. The foods they deliver to our table are beautiful to behold, a joy to cook and eat, are high in nutritive value and are without chemical residue. Our support of these dedicated farmers yields healthier ingredients, strengthens our sense of local community, builds our local economy and, most importantly, it is a vital step toward protecting these resources for future generations.

"The cuisine here at 'Higgins' is truly rooted in our Northwest soil. We hope our commitment to these principles of ingredients, which are local, seasonal, organic and sustainable, will nourish your mind and body. Please help by supporting our local organic farmers when you shop for your kitchen. Their fruits and vegetables represent so much more than just good flavor — they are the seeds of our future."

Three decades years later, the essay still fills the back of Higgins' menus.

"We knew that commitment was going to be our thing," Higgins said. "To this day, it hasn't changed. We stay true to that, because that's really important."

Higgins has drawn from some of the same local producers for the last 30 years. Individual contributors supply grass-fed beef and pork, oysters, fish, poultry, tomatoes, mushrooms, and more. A gardener himself, Higgins became an expert in what to grow in a Northwest climate and when, knowledge he'd often pass on to others. Farmers markets, sparse in the 1980s, began to flourish, with individual growers paying attention to what professional and casual chefs wanted.

"At the markets, it's a self-governing system," Higgins said, "Everybody realizes that if I grow everything that they're growing, I'm not going to sell a new one or neither one of us is going to do well. So people start figuring out that the real opportunities are in the different products for diversity, and also in extended seasons."

With its proximity to Portland's performance theaters, the restaurant became a local favorite. Higgins remembers

Greg Higgins (second from right) and his staff welcome Julia Child.
(Photo courtesy of Greg Higgins)

James DePriest, nationally acclaimed conductor of the Oregon Symphony, came in often enough that the staff got him his own oversized chair to accommodate his size.

"Bud Clark used to come in for lunch all the time," Higgins said of the former mayor. "He'd ride his bike up, come in and he'd sit at the bar. No matter what it was, every day, he would order something off the menu or a special and he would stand up on his stool, those tall stools at the bar, and take a picture. I'd be like, 'I can't have the mayor falling off his stool and getting hurt in my bar, man.' But that was the way it was."

Higgins became a national voice for sustainable cuisine, as a founding member and head of the Portland chapter of Chefs Collaborative, which celebrated "the joys of local, seasonal, and artisanal cooking." After being nominated three years in a row, he received a 2002 James Beard Award for Best Chef in the Northwest. Fittingly for one dedicated to new approaches, he spent too much time at the shop of a particularly intriguing butcher in New York's Hudson Valley and missed the ceremony in the city.

"The validation really was for my crew," he said. "I got back from the trip and when I came back into the restaurant, the whole place just went bonkers. Because they are the people that earned it. I'm just steering the ship and teaching. If they don't execute, that never happens."

Though Higgins Restaurant is known for the continuity of its staff, several former employees went on to either own or cook in well-known Portland restaurants, including Ciao Vito, Trifecta, and Park Kitchen. "There's a little of me all over the place," Higgins said.

All along, he realized his vision, creating and running a restaurant of his own the way he wanted, and contributing to Portland's emergence as a dining stalwart. As most of Portland's top restaurants when he opened his doors are gone, Higgins keeps on cooking.

"I'm not giving it up," he said. "So as long as people come, we'll feed them."

29

A Welcome Return

AS MUCH AS ANYONE IN the 1990s, Cory Schreiber promoted Northwest cuisine and the conditions that allowed it to thrive in Portland's restaurants. A decade earlier, he rightfully had his doubts.

By the time he was old enough to drink, Schreiber already was a seasoned veteran of the Portland restaurant scene. At age 11, he began working at Dan & Louis Oyster Bar, the restaurant in Portland's Old Town that his great-grandfather opened more than 50 years earlier. He worked briefly in a Mexican fast-food restaurant when he was 17, then at the London Grill in the Benson Hotel, first as a busboy then as a chef's apprentice.

Among his learnings, Schreiber knew that the restaurant landscape in Portland was no place for a young, aspiring chef. He left in 1982.

"I can't say from the standpoint of other professions," he said, "but from a culinary standpoint, there was nothing."

Backed by classical European cooking training and experience at the London Grill, Schreiber worked in restaurants and hotels in San Francisco, Boston, Chicago, and back to San Francisco, where he became the first executive chef of the acclaimed Cypress Club.

All the while, regular visits to his hometown kept Schreiber abreast of Portland's evolving dining scene. He spoke of a watershed moment in 1993 when he was dining outside at Zefiro, which had burst on the scene a few years earlier.

"Money in Portland was always kind of hidden," he said. "I looked over and there was a bottle of Pouilly-Fuissé, a $60 bottle of wine, on a table in the open. It just occurred to me like, 'Wow, this city is changing. You can show money now.' I remember that so clearly. I was like, 'Okay, it's time to come.'"

Six months later, Schreiber signed a lease for Wildwood, his restaurant on Northwest 21st Avenue. His commitment to locally sourced ingredients and the creative dishes they encouraged quickly helped the restaurant emerge as a Portland favorite. It was named *The Oregonian's* Restaurant of the Year for 1995, the year after it opened.

"Schreiber has injected enthusiasm and style into the Portland food scene, where he already has emerged as a major player," *The Oregonian* wrote.

Schreiber learned early on that not only was it an advantage for Portland chefs to use local ingredients, it was essential to talk about it. His classical training led to written menus that described how food was prepared—roasted, grilled, poached, and so on. A marketer quickly suggested that the menu should emphasize where the food was from.

"When we did start to get very specific about where the zucchini came from, or what farm, or from Hood River or Columbia River, or whatever it was, that's when the customers took notice," he said. "Surely, if it came in good, it tasted good. I'll give ourselves some credit. But I really would give the credit to the farmers. So I realized within the first year or two that we needed to continue to talk about that and make it part of our story because that was the draw factor."

One of the first things he did for Wildwood was to buy a pickup truck to collect so much of the Oregon bounty that would end up on diners' plates. He hired a buyer who worked 70-80 hours a week, spending as much as 20 hours a week in the truck visiting farms, as well as local outlets such as Sheridan Fruit Company, Nicky USA for game and meats, and Western Union Farms for berries. Schreiber estimates that at the high time of year, he'd purchase from as many as 25 different purveyors.

"I never viewed it as extreme at the time, because I think it gets back to the point that the abundance was so wide, so available, like why wouldn't you just embrace and engage in all of it," he said. "Especially from a chef standpoint, there was the notion that we were sending a message to the rest of the country and trying to draw cooks and servers and bartenders here."

Schreiber also realized something else. In the mid-1990s, business travelers and vacationers alike were hungry for what the city had to offer. Portland had become a draw.

Cory Schreiber made Wildwood a go-to restaurant starting in 1994. (Jerry Hart photo courtesy of Cory Schreiber)

"You could track where the users of the Visas and the Mastercards and American Express cards were from," he said. "Half were not from Portland. We were feeding off Chicago, San Francisco, Los Angeles, Seattle. That became half our clientele."

The restaurant's décor featured a wall mural honoring James Beard, a Portland-born devotee of Northwest cuisine and the forerunner of today's celebrity chefs. Several phrases from Beard's memoir, *Delights and Prejudices*, were noted on the mural, drawing the attention of a senior diner who called Schreiber over.

"Why is my mother's name on this mural?" she asked. The diner, Mary Hamblet, had known Beard since they were children in the early 1900s and their families spent summer times together at the Oregon Coast. Schreiber and Hamblet quickly became good friends.

"She's the one who kind of gave me a first-hand account of growing up with Beard," he said. "For me, it was getting to know Beard through the localized version. It wasn't the New York version."

So in 1998, when Schreiber became the first Portland chef to win a coveted James Beard Award, he felt even more of a connection to the man known as the Dean of American Cooking. They shared similar backgrounds, with Beard learning to love Oregon seafood during his childhood summers in Gearhart, and Schreiber, a fifth-generation restaurateur, having spent his summers working the family oyster farm near Yaquina Bay.

"I felt very proud that I was the first chef to bring it to Portland," he said of the award. "To me that was indicative of my ancestry. I felt there was a direct connection there."

By the mid-1990s, Portland's top chefs all were placing a strong focus on locally sourced food, but it was Schreiber who wrote the book. *Wildwood: Cooking from the Source in the Pacific Northwest* was published in 2000. It mixes stories of Schreiber's background with recipes from the region and even has a chapter devoted to Beard and his recipes.

It was one of many efforts by Schreiber to evangelize the cooking and restaurants in the area he left as a young man. Progress drew him back.

"I can look at legacy with my own family and figure it's a bloodline. It's a pedigree," he said. "I never knew anything else. I never wanted to do anything. But it hit me pretty hard. Yeah, this was my path."

And another thing…

One summer night at Wildwood, a couple sat at an outside table, preferring to stay in the dark. Looking at the menu by candlelight, the man didn't see what he wanted, which did not dissuade him. He wanted a Caprese salad.

It was actor Robert DeNiro. Yep, Travis Bickle from Taxi Driver, Vito Corleone from Godfather II, and Jimmy Conway from Goodfellas made his request.

Can't you hear him? "What did I say? What did I say? Make me a Caprese salad."

"Thank God it was August," owner Cory Schreiber said. "Because we had tomatoes."

······ **30** ······

A Food City Rises

"IF A CITY COULD BE designed by chefs, Portland might be the result," *The New York Times* roared in the summer of 1995.

"Ringed by mountains, pristine rivers, woods and fields, and the Pacific Ocean," the story went on, "Oregon is a virtual food laboratory."

Word was out on Portland's farm-to-table approach to cooking, and the tantalizing dishes it created. In addition to the emergence of restaurants such as Zefiro, Higgins, and Wildwood, the International Pinot Noir Celebration, which started in 1987, brought Northwest chefs and prominent journalists together in nearby McMinnville for an annual weekend of wine, food, and shared ideas.

"It was like smoke and mirrors for the first few years, but it got a huge amount of attention," said Greg Higgins, an original chef at the event. "We started inviting a lot of guest chefs, and then the word got out. I really think that was a big catalyst. Naturally, they'd see the same things I did. They'd look around and say, 'Wow, there's lots of opportunity here.'"

Portland's opportunity called out to a husband-and-wife team who would bring excitement to the local restaurant scene for a generation. Vitaly and Kimberly Paley met in New York while both were pursuing other careers, he as a concert pianist and she as a modern dancer. Vitaly, born in Belarus, and Kimberly, a Californian, worked side jobs in the food industry in New York City.

Looking beyond their time in the performing arts, they both got more interested in food and wine. The couple took a 10-month trip to France and apprenticed in a two-star Michelin Restaurant, he in the kitchen, she with the sommelier. From there, they decided to pursue their passion for food in Portland "on a one-way ticket with no plan."

"Oregon reminded us of France, where ingredients are the stars," Vitaly Paley wrote in *The Paley's Place Cookbook: Recipes and stories from the Pacific Northwest.*

Initially, Vitaly worked the line at Pazzo in the Vintage Plaza Hotel and Kimberly staffed the front of house at recently opened Wildwood. They also dined at Zefiro and saw potential for what they wanted to do. When they talked to Wildwood owner Cory Schreiber about an idea to open a restaurant on the Oregon coast, he advised against it. Instead, the Paleys bought a small Victorian-style house across the street from Wildwood and opened Paley's Place in February 1995.

"I think we invited about 30 people and it was nice and lively. It felt really great," Vitaly told a local TV station 26 years later. "The next day, there were only two people in the dining room, and they were Kimberly's parents."

But Paley's Place quickly caught on as yet another farm-to-table restaurant in Portland, this one featuring Vitaly's French-influenced cooking and personalized service that included amuse-bouche for each diner and handmade chocolate with the bill.

The Times raved over Paley's just five months after it opened, touting the "seasonal menu of such specialties as goat cheese and arugula-like rocket greens, from farms just a short bicycle ride from the restaurant, and purple spinach ravioli. Truffled risotto with thick wedges of porcini, flavored with Monterey Jack cheese, is as earthy as a hike in the Cascades."

Paley's, Wildwood, and Zefiro made Northwest 21st Avenue Portland's go-to dining destination, while on Southwest Broadway, Philippe Boulot was gaining notice at the Heathman Hotel. Boulot, born and trained in France, was working in New York City before taking over when Higgins left to open his own restaurant.

Boulot had worked under legendary chef Joel Robuchon in France and welcomed the opportunity to work at a larger restaurant where he could control the concept. "I wanted to be a chef, and a food and beverage manager as well," he told *Portland Food and Drink* in 2006. "So, I needed a place big enough and small enough to do this."

The Heathman and Boulot were an ideal match. With its formal French-inspired menu and extensive wine list, the Heathman took its place as a special-occasion destination or a pre-theater stop adjacent to the Arlene Schnitzer Concert Hall.

In its story celebrating the abundance of ingredients Portland chefs had to work with, *The Times* praised the Heathman, writing "A superb veal chop from a local farm is paired with a sweet fricassee of Walla Walla onions and porcini. Local morels are in season for much of the summer, and they show up in every conceivable form."

Boulot received the James Beard Award for the Best Chef in the Northwest in 2001. Higgins won the following year and Paley in 2005, joining 1998 winner Schreiber in an impressive run for Portland chefs at "The Oscars of Food." They all put their creative spin on what would become known as Northwest cuisine.

Moreover, they all contributed to Portland's transition from the hit-and-miss-miss-miss 1980s to a nationally recognized dining destination, one that inspired a new generation of chefs and restaurateurs that have treated diners well into the 21st century. It's a legacy the stalwarts of the '90s are proud of.

"Besides all the bounty and beauty we have here, it became a dining destination," Kimberly Paley told KOIN 6 News. "People came to see Multnomah Falls and go to the coast and do that and they came to dine in Portland, and that was exciting to be part of that movement."

····· **31** ·····

Changing the Ad Game

BY THE EARLY 1990S, WIEDEN+KENNEDY'S success earned the agency an ongoing mix of praise, dismissal, and allure.

On one hand, some in the industry doubted that a small agency in a small city could compete in the long run. One senior executive of an established New York agency told *The New York Times* in 1990, "Cities like New York and Chicago have great talent pools to draw from; Portland does not. A small agency in Portland will never be a big player in this business."

A few months later, Wieden+Kennedy was named the 1991 Agency of Year by *Advertising Age* "for its artistry in creating and maintaining creative momentum during an economic recession."

Sure, said the naysayers, anyone could make great ads for Nike, but could Wieden+Kennedy do the same for others? W+K countered that charge when it landed the Subaru account and opened a Philadelphia office in 1991, only to lose the account and close the office two years later.

If there was one key group that had come to greatly admire the agency's work, it was other creatives. The first generation of W+K copywriters and art directors attracted others.

"I'd worked at some good agencies in New York, but Wieden was still kind of a gold standard," said copywriter Hank Perlman. "Everybody was jealous of Wieden's work. I mean, it was just that much better."

Perlman, then 27, was drawn to Portland and W+K in 1993 on the promise of freelance work. While most of those who came to Wieden were hoping to work on the Nike account, Perlman was happy to be assigned to the agency's newest client, ESPN. He helped promote the network's hockey and football coverage before a brief diversion to help with W+K's pitch on the Microsoft account. A contingency from the agency took a bus to Redmond, outside of Seattle, to present to Bill Gates, but when they landed the account, Perlman wanted off, so he approached agency co-founder Dan Wieden.

"I went into his office and I just basically begged him," Perlman said. "I said 'I'm sorry, but I really want to work on ESPN.' He was nice enough to let me. He knew my heart wasn't in it."

The marriage of Wieden+Kennedy and Microsoft, a cultural mismatch if ever there was one, lasted five challenging years. Perlman stayed on ESPN and helped create one of the most memorable and long-lasting campaigns in advertising history.

"This is SportsCenter" celebrated the network's flagship program, which delivered comprehensive daily sports highlights at a time before the Internet showed slam dunks and home runs seemingly before the ball hit the ground. It was appointment viewing for passionate sports fans as much for the on-air personalities as for the highlights.

The journey to "This is SportsCenter" began with a trip by Perlman and art director Rick McQuiston to Bristol, Connecticut. The duo spent five days at ESPN headquarters observing the culture and operations.

"It's the middle of nowhere," Perlman said. "At the time, ESPN felt like a glorified college radio station. We couldn't believe it, because you're watching *SportsCenter* and you just think this is sort of the center of the sports universe. But the reality is, it's like this trailer park with kind of a rundown office building where they put the whole thing together."

The show blended serious journalism with casual humor for a devoted audience. But the world in which it was created deserved something better, even if it was made up.

"So the logical extension for us was, if it's this goofy and funny on the air, imagine how crazy it could be around *SportsCenter* when they're off the air," McQuiston explained in an early interview. "So we set about creating this alternate world, much as they did for 'Spinal Tap.' From there, we could do almost anything. It was wide open, which is perfect for a creative."

This is Spinal Tap was a 1984 mockumentary following the travails of a British metal rock band. As a nod to the inspiration for the campaign, Michael McKean reprised his role as Spinal Tap guitarist David St. Hubens, who in one spot demonstrated his recommended riffs for *SportsCenter* and other sports.

The ESPN universe Perlman and McQuiston created was one where athletes, mascots, and sports anchors all worked together in an office setting. It felt perfectly normal for gold-medal winning gymnast Mary Lou Retton to perform a series of front handsprings down the office hall as she looked for the copy machine, or for NBA assist leader Jason Kidd to fly in on a helicopter to pass off highlight tapes for broadcast. After a tough show, anchor Dan Patrick cheered himself up listening to basketball star Grant Hill play piano in the lobby, even dropping a couple of bucks in his tip jar. Anchor Scott Van Pelt couldn't understand why mascots, marching bands, rodeo cowboys, and others were sprinting past his cube, until he read his email alerting staff to leftover muffins and bagels in the conference room.

The possibilities were endless, and with ESPN owning its own network, so was airtime. Shot with few frills in a documentary style, the first 70 spots cost a reported $1 million to produce.

"We had a lot of fun making the commercials," Perlman said. "It almost did, at times, feel like working on *Saturday Night Live* or something where ideas were kind of at the last minute. An athlete would show up, and they wouldn't necessarily like the idea we gave them, so we would come up with a new idea. Or we didn't necessarily always show the athletes the ideas beforehand, so they would show up and we would pitch this and say, 'What if we tried this?' And they'd say, 'Okay, that sounds funny.' We were kind of allowed a lot of freedom to do whatever we wanted."

Usually, but not always. When the Walt Disney Company acquired ESPN in 1996, the creative team figured it had a natural tie-in. The spot opened with assurances that the purchase would not affect programming, then jumped to anchors wearing mouse ears and Tinker Bell flying across the screen.

"We of course thought that was really funny," Perlman said. "But nobody at Disney thought that was funny."

The campaign's success no doubt contributed to Wieden+Kennedy's continued growth. In addition to Microsoft, the agency added Coca-Cola and, for a couple years, Miller Beer. Nike took much of its business away in 1997, but would return in '99, by which time Wieden+Kennedy had offices in Portland, New York, Amsterdam, London, and Tokyo. The agency had become a major player in the advertising industry.

"This is SportsCenter," won industry awards and made many best-of lists, including the top television campaign of the 1990s by the One Club for Art and Copy, a group of more than 1,000 members. The campaign long outlived Perlman's three-year tenure with Wieden+Kennedy, as he took advantage of professional opportunities and moved back to New York.

"You don't always appreciate it at that time, but it did feel like a pretty special time," he said of his stay in Portland. "When you look back at it, it was such a great group of people. It was so fun, and it was so creative."

Those who were there credit the company's founders, Dan Wieden and David Kennedy, for making it possible for creative people to flourish.

"They created a culture where they could do the best work of their lives," Dave Luhr, the agency's former president, said at Wieden's 2022 memorial. "They attracted talent to this weird city and pushed people to grow and rise above expectations."

And another thing...

The "This is SportsCenter" campaign was a hit from the beginning, for viewers and critics. In fact, the first year's worth of spots won a 1995 Sports Emmy Award for Promotions. When art director Rick McQuiston opened the package containing the Emmy at the Wieden+Kennedy office, it set off a spontaneous party in nearby bars.

"For two or three hours, the entire agency was out celebrating. The agency bought all the alcohol, all the food. It was huge," said Janet Champ, the copywriter who was married to McQuiston. "In the beginning there were about 60 of us. And then by the time we finished there were probably about 110, 120 people."

Champ remembers stops at Kells Irish Pub, Kelly's Olympian, and McCormick & Schmick's on Southwest 1st Avenue, where the Emmy got left behind and had to be retrieved at closing time.

32

Dining With a Twist of Cool

BRUCE CAREY JOKINGLY CALLED IT a midlife crisis. For Brad Cloepfil, it was a career birth.

It was Saucebox, a restaurant that invited new levels of creativity to the Portland dining scene. It opened in the fall of 1995 with the aim of being a hip, cool spot that Carey unabashedly predicted would be "completely unlike anything that people in Portland have seen."

Carey warranted attention. He, along with partners Chris Israel and Monique Siu, opened Zefiro in 1990. It, too, was unlike anything previously seen in Portland, with its art-filled design, cool vibe, and eclectic Mediterranean-inspired menu. Cloepfil, in Portland trying to ignite a career in architecture, was among Zefiro's admirers.

"That's where everybody went," he said. "There are those times in history where you read about that café or

that bar where everyone goes and you think, 'I'd give anything to have been alive.' Then that happened."

It was a far cry from his early years, when Cloepfil was
part of the exodus of young, creative people from Portland
in the 1970s. A graduate of Tigard High School and the
University of Oregon, he worked for famed architect Mario
Botta in Switzerland and got his graduate degree from
Columbia University in New York. By the mid-1980s, he
noticed, Portland was changing for the better.

"Things were starting to happen in Portland. It was kind
of getting exciting," he said. "So I thought, 'Well, let's move
back and see if I can start my own office.'"

Cloepfil's first office space was on Northwest 5th Avenue,
between Couch and Davis, where he shared the top floor
with noted artist Mel Katz.

"I had a whole half of a floor, thousands of square feet,
and maybe it was $150," he said. "But there was no heat,
so I had those oil radiators. That's when I started smoking
cigars, because it was freezing. So, internal comfort."

Cloepfil gained experience working for others, and made
ends meet by teaching. In 1994, he opened Allied Works
Architecture, around the time Carey and Israel were looking for another opportunity beyond Zefiro. Cloepfil's assistant, Mindy Holdsworth, introduced him to Carey.

"I told Mindy I would do anything for those guys, Chris
and Bruce, because they obviously get it," Clopefil said.
"It's like, 'Who's doing things at the very highest level and
aspires to the highest level?' It was those guys."

Carey and Israel leased the former Mexican Café on
Southwest Broadway with no plans for a big redesign, until

they met with Cloepfil. "We got into it and I just started showing them. I just said this is what it could be," Cloepfil recalled. "Then they got really excited."

The project came at a key time for its owners. Zefiro had been an enormous success, but the long hours were taking their toll. Israel took a year sabbatical, which included four months traveling in Asia. Carey, too, was ready for something new.

"I think of Zefiro as the firstborn favorite child that reflected where we were at that time, personally," he said. "And in that same way, when we opened Saucebox in 1995, we were maybe a little bit young for a midlife crisis, but it felt like a party place."

Carey's vision for kind of a Manhattan-meets-Tokyo club vibe had to adjust quickly. The cocktail nation crowd trended toward late night. The deejay, which had been planned for every open hour, shifted with it.

The menu benefited from Israel's travels to Japan, Taiwan, and Thailand, where he ate at restaurants, food carts, and in homes. He went to local markets and riffed off local recipes. Spring rolls, salad rolls, dumplings, and curries aligned with Asian-inspired seafood entrees that took advantage of Portland's local fare.

The New York Times called it "the absolute best of East meets West." After Israel left town again, this time for New York, chef Jeff McMahon stepped in. *The Oregonian* named Saucebox its Restaurant of the Year in 1998, saying, "The food is even cooler than the crowd."

At any hour, Saucebox *was* cool. The darkened entry, the lighting around the bar, the lofted dining space, and

Glitzy Saucebox gave Portland citizenship in Cocktail Nation.
(Photo courtesy of Allied Works Architecture)

even the co-ed sink area in the bathrooms made you feel like you were somewhere special, yet comfortably so.

For his design efforts, Cloepfil was paid $2,000 in cash and $2,000 in bar credit, which he says he's sure he never reached. The true reward for his work at Saucebox would come a few years later. But that's another story for another chapter.

33

A New Voice Emerges

IN ITS EARLY DAYS, WIEDEN+KENNEDY'S growing reputation as one of the most creative ad agencies in the country surprised many in the industry. The reason? Its location.

Appearing alongside Dan Wieden at the Cannes Lions International Festival of Creativity in 2012, Sir John Hegarty recalled his reaction to an early W+K ad for Nike. The co-founder of London-based ad agency Barter Bogle Hegarty described seeking out a map in an effort to find Portland.

"Up there? My God, how can you run a great agency out of Portland, Oregon? Finding it was hard enough," he said. "I just thought from that moment on, seeing that work and seeing what they were doing in that place, to me kind of said there's something special going on here. Because if you can run a great agency from Portland, Oregon, it goes against all the things people believe about creativity needing to be congregated in certain places."

W+K played on with its unconventional approach to gaining the attention of consumers. In fact, when turning its attention to women in campaigns for Nike, the agency did some of its most memorable, impactful work.

Women had been part of several early Nike ads. Some of the first "Just Do It" spots featured Stacy Allison, the first American woman to climb to the top of Mount Everest, and Priscilla Welch, a runner who won the women's division of the 1987 New York City Marathon at age 42. Women were among the everyday athletes in "Revolution" and Joan Benoit helped out the cross-training campaign by saying "Bo knows running."

But one spot stood out as evidence that Wieden+Kennedy, and therefore Nike, were missing the mark in earlier efforts. In it, triathlete Joanne Ernst was supposed to inspire women to work out. Her closing line ("It wouldn't hurt if you stopped eating like a pig.") proved more insulting than inspiring. That the line was written by a man and approved by several others would lead to a series of ground-breaking ads written by Janet Champ.

Champ, the admin-turned-copywriter whose first commercial was "Revolution," was in her office with art director Charlotte Moore when Dan Wieden dropped by.

"He stuck his head in and he said, 'Well, you guys are girls,'" Champ recalled. "And we looked up and said, 'Uh huh.' And he said, 'Great. I'm going to put you on the Nike women's fitness work.' He closed the door and walked on, and I worked on it for seven years straight."

Champ and Moore started by exploring how women were being talked to in ads appearing in such publications as *Cosmopolitan* and *Glamour.* Their response appeared in their first effort, called "List," in 1990. On the left column, a dozen wardrobe tips included, "Your 48-Hour Bra," "Your Support Pantyhose," and "Your Dress With The Vertical Stripes." The right side said, simply, "Self-Support From Nike. Just Do It."

The tone of women's advertising at Nike had shifted, and the company saw sales of women's product increase significantly. As a 2006 retrospective in *Advertising & Society Review* said, the women at W+K "took on a patriarchal company's advertising, hijacked it for feminism, and did it in style."

Champ recalled that "when Charlotte and I got done reading these (women's) magazines, which we hadn't seen since high school, she said, 'I got an idea. Why don't you just write a woman's life?'"

Champ's copy was poetic, insightful and encouraging. One passage bemoaned that women are often measured by curves and numbers, "by all the outside things that don't ever add up to who she is on the inside." Another describes the girl finally reaching the top of the rope in gym class, "And there is absolutely nowhere to go but up." Another acknowledged that it was okay for a woman to take care of herself, for herself, "Because you know it's never too late to have a life. And never too late to change one."

They produced an eight-page magazine insert, an extremely unusual approach. It had no pictures of shoes, instead featuring photos of young girls and grown women, including Champ's mom.

"We called it the dialogue campaign," Champ said in a 2015 interview. "The one thing you don't do is shove a shoe in someone's face and say 'buy my shoe.' You say, 'I'm like you, I get you, I know you, let's talk about this.'"

The women took their booklet to their bosses. They were sure Dan Wieden, a word guy, would love it. They were less certain about David Kennedy, a designer at heart.

"He kept looking at it. He didn't say anything for like five minutes, and I thought I was going to die," Champ said. "Then suddenly, he said, 'Well, once again, I don't know what this is, because this isn't advertising. But I fucking love it.'"

So did the women who responded with hundreds of calls to Nike and W+K to praise the campaign, which continued for several years. When the prestigious One Club for Art and Copy chose its top 10 print campaigns of the entire 1990s, the Nike women's campaign finished second.

"Calling (Champ's) work copy falls short," Scott Bedbury, Nike's head of advertising at the time, told *The Oregonian.* "It's poetry that still stops people in their tracks 25 years later."

Then came the biggest success yet. When Nike pushed the agency for something provocative and surprising, it was time for another all-teams approach, where the best idea would rise. Champ suggested Janet Jackson as Venus Blackmon, a counter to Spike Lee's Mars Blackmon character. That didn't fly.

Instead, more than 20 years after the passage of Title IX, the winning concept portrayed young girls speaking of the importance of sports in their lives. Based on statistics Nike had gathered, the girls pointed out that if they could play sports, "I will suffer less depression," and "I will be 60 percent less likely to get breast cancer," and "I will be more likely to leave a man who beats me."

"If You Let Me Play" came out in 1995 and was a huge hit, drawing thousands of letters and calls to Nike, including those from tearful mothers grateful for the important message to their daughters. A generation later, women's sports are thriving, and the notion of "letting girls play sports," is almost an afterthought. The ad won a One Show Gold Pencil award for Champ and art director Rachel Manganiello, and put to rest that W+K didn't know how to talk to women.

The agency from the little town in the Northwest corner of the U.S. had become accustomed to success. By then, Wieden+Kennedy was a major attraction, drawing creative talent from all over to Portland to do some of the industry's finest work.

"They were all these different people, eclectic people, interesting people, talented people, fun people," Champ said. "Still to this day, it's like we're all stepbrothers and stepsisters and cousins."

Champ left the agency in 1999, embarking on a successful freelance career. She has never forgotten the early lessons she learned at Wieden+Kennedy.

"It was always, anything's possible, and that's because they started the agency with that thought," she said. "It was, we don't want to do advertising. We want to change the world kind of stuff. It just made you believe you could do it too."

······ 34 ······

A Leap Forward for the Arts

ONE OF THE MOST DYNAMIC hubs of creative expression that emerged in Portland in the 1990s was the Portland Institute for Contemporary Art. Part theater for national and international figures and part nurturing ground for local talent, PICA grew out of a change in direction at the city's more established art institution.

The road to PICA began when Kristy Edmunds hit a dead end at the Portland Art Museum. Established in 1892, the museum had a traditional approach with a focus on gathering and showing the works of historically significant visual artists. A move to include more contemporary art under curator John Weber and, eventually Edmunds, stalled when Weber left in 1993. When executive director John Buchanan took over the financially struggling museum and emphasized raising capital over nurturing contemporary art, Edmunds departed.

If not for a love for her adopted home, Edmunds might have left for a larger city and built-in opportunity. Raised near Lake Chelan, Washington, and, for a few years, in Minneapolis, she came to Portland in her early 20s. It was the late 1980s, and as opposed to a decade earlier, young people had reasons to want to be in Portland.

"It was a city I felt I could believe in," she said. "You know, I understood that there was a growth boundary, I understood that there was a skycap, I understood that there were intentional short blocks, I understood that there were different kinds of parks and green spaces that were there. Forest Park, to me, it was this miracle. Where does that kind of thing ever happen? And there was a planning and anticipation of doing something differently with a kind of optimism about the future. It made me feel like there was some kind of authorship around a future that I was interested in."

Her departure from the museum meant it was time to author a new chapter. With the closing of the Portland Center for the Visual Arts in 1987 and the Northwest Artists Workshop two years later, the viability of nimble, privately supported artistic endeavors was in question when Edmunds thought about starting PICA.

"Oh, it wasn't viable," she laughed. "The only thing that was viable was optimism, hopefulness, and a certain amount of trust that had been established nationally and regionally with artists and a handful of patrons."

A small group of supporters that included contemporary art gallery owners Elizabeth Leach, Rod Pulliam, and

Victoria Frey encouraged Edmunds to give it a try, believing in her cause and her skills.

"Big-league talent. Big-league vision," said Randy Gragg, former art critic for *The Oregonian*. "Kristy was just very charismatic. She was a really, really important influence in terms of cultivating that kind of alternative energy."

Edmunds became known as a tireless advocate for contemporary art in Portland. Before launching PICA, she first had to overcome a sales pitch from another Portland force, ad executive Dan Wieden.

Wieden's interest in Edmunds was to inspire his employees in an unconventional way. "I've always had this dream of creating a place where people in our business could work alongside artists," he told *The Oregonian*. "At the end of the day, creativity is creativity. And some of the most inspiring people around are artists."

During lunch at Jake's Famous Crawfish, the venerable Portland seafood restaurant, Wieden offered Edmunds a job. She admits that the offer left the clam chowder shaking in her spoon.

"He quoted me a salary," Edmunds said. "I was like, 'Dude, I just started this not-for-profit organization, and in a weird way, it's trying to do the exact same thing, but not from a commercial or corporate angle. And the salary that you just quoted me is like my annual budget for PICA.'"

Edmunds went on to describe an entity that would inspire and even challenge a broader public audience while elevating Portland's status as a creative city. Passing on the job, Edmunds earned Wieden's support and eventual patronage during a period when government funding for the arts had diminished.

With a first-year budget of around $160,000, PICA opened its doors in 1995. At least it would have if it had doors. In PICA's early days, Edmunds ran the organization from a corner space at Boora Architects. Performances were staged in various small theaters, and art exhibitions took place in vacant warehouses, a nomadic existence that added to PICA's cool factor.

Pearl District developer Al Solheim would help find, and in some cases, donate exhibition space. Sound engineer Bill Bose and lighting expert T.C. Smith would pitch in with their expertise, with the latter even helping to hang lights.

"Then you'd go to pay him and he wouldn't leave you an invoice," Edmunds said of Smith. "He'd just ask for a six-pack of Guinness."

PICA's earliest events included a show from an experimental dance group led by New York choreographer Stephanie Skura. An installation called "Pushing Image Paradigms" took place in a recently closed tire wholesaler under the Fremont Bridge and featured the work of 11 photographers from around the world. Performance artists Spalding Gray and Rinde Eckert each visited and French artist Francis Alys punctured a full paint can, then took to the streets to make his mark.

Eventually, the event that gained the most notoriety was the annual Dada Ball, a fundraiser known for the outrageous outfits worn by guests as they celebrated artistic freedom.

"Its brand identity was actually bigger than PICA's," Edmunds said. "We had people flying in from all over the country for that thing. And people would discover something about Portland that they just didn't know."

In a sense, that was the unspoken mission of PICA: to showcase Portland's creative environment, both to those who lived here and those who visited. Edmunds developed a bustling network of volunteers to support PICA and provide a showcase for the city.

"A city that is welcoming of creativity, you can feel it," Edmunds said. "You feel it in food, pubs, streets, various kinds of things. And if you're a creative person, you want to be around other creative communities. Most artists are really, regardless of their art form, generous to place. So how you could help the city thrive was super important to us all."

By 2000, with the first three years offered rent free, PICA moved into the ground floor of the new Wieden+Kennedy building at Northwest 13th Avenue and Everett Street. An exhibition space, library and offices gave PICA a formal home, but critics said the loss of the traveling shows stole some of PICA's spirit. The dotcom bust and a post-9/11 economy also contributed to diminished support from a new generation of Portland professionals who had been contributors.

Edmunds left Portland in 2005 to become the artistic director of the Melbourne International Arts Festival. Frey, former owner of the Quartersaw Gallery, took over as executive director and remained until 2022. PICA's evolution included a relocation to Portland's Eliot neighborhood while continuing to support and showcase contemporary art.

Looking back, Edmunds credits Portland with nurturing her exploration of creative possibilities, as well as resilience to do what it takes to break the mold.

"A maverick sensibility is often untrusted, and in Portland, it is trusted," she said. "So even though people aren't necessarily going to join you on your journey, they don't block that from happening or isolate you. There's enough suspension of disbelief that things can actually fall forward. And once they start to fall forward, they become familiar and people sometimes realize, 'Wow, that was great.' And it becomes easier for the next idea that comes forward."

······ **35** ······

This Place Was Hopping

IT SEEMS HARD TO BELIEVE in the hop-infused Portland of today, but there was a time that India Pale Ale was a foreign term to local beer lovers.

"Can you imagine going to a bar in 1996 and there are no IPAs on tap?" brewer Karl Ockert asked. "There were lots of amber ales, lots of fruit and wheat beers, but not a single IPA."

IPA had to come a long way to gain prominence in Portland pubs. The term dated to the 1800s, named for the British approach of adding extra hops as a preservative for beer being shipped to various locations, including India. The evolution of American IPAs included efforts in New Jersey, California, and Washington.

But it took the scent of desperation for the style to come to Portland. Dick and Nancy Ponzi, owners of Bridgeport

Brewing since it opened in 1984, sold the pioneering brewery in 1995 to the Texas-based Gambrinus company, whose products included Corona and Shiner Bock. As he returned his focus to his winery, Dick Ponzi admitted that his brewery had lost traction as the market he helped nurture grew more competitive.

Gambrinus founder Carlos Alvarez turned to one of his executives, Phil Sexton of Australia, to suggest an approach to a beer that might find new inroads. Sexton correctly pointed out that the Northwest was one of the great hop producers in the world, and experimenting with an IPA would be worth a try.

"I hadn't actually had an IPA," Sexton admitted to *Willamette Week* in 2014. "I had just read about them in old brewing texts."

Ockert, Bridgeport's original brewmaster, had left the company in 1990. He returned in '96, just in time to help with the new formulation.

"It wasn't my idea, and I didn't invent it," Ockert said. "But I was part of a team that put it together and then I helped fine tune it."

With its combination of five different hops varieties, the result was a floral, citrus-tinged delight with what today would be considered mild hop presence. Bridgeport IPA became the signature product the new owner wanted.

"Bridgeport IPA was a hell of a beer. It was just super popular right off the get go," Ockert said. "We thought it was going to be a niche beer for us, but it turned out to be almost instantly our best seller."

Critics loved it too. The beer won a gold medal at Denver's Great American Beer Festival in 1997 and in 2000 it became the first American beer in the more-than 100-year history of the prestigious Brewing Industry International Awards in England to win the international ale category.

Gary Geist, a former Bridgeport employee and co-founder of the Lucky Labrador Brewing Company, called it "a total game-changer." The beer set a new course for Portland brewers for years to come.

"Bridgeport IPA was the beer that made Portland into an IPA town," writer John Foyston told *Willamette Week*. "And it probably started the hop wars, too."

In many cases, balanced IPAs gave way to uber-hopped beers that bartenders might warn "will burn your face off." In addition, Portland's adventurous brewers continued to seek and offer the next big thing, which turned out to be a mixed bag for Bridgeport.

"Back in the early '80s, we were just trying to get a beachhead going," Ockert said. "So we were just imitating English beers and Old World beers and now we've gone way beyond that. The palette is endless. So there's a huge amount of creativity available."

Bridgeport lasted until 2019, when it closed its original pub at Northwest 13th and Marshall and ceased brewing operations. It was the end of an era.

"They say that men can't have babies, so they start businesses. For me, Bridgeport was my baby," said Ockert, now a brewing industry consultant. "I was so sorry to see it go."

And another thing…

Long before a 21st-century makeover brought it in line with the rest of the sparkling Pearl District, the Bridgeport Brew Pub was a no-frills oasis amid abandoned warehouses and pothole-littered streets. It was known for its dependable variety of craft beers, tasty slices of pizza served on paper plates , and a picnic-table seating.

And, at least for the men in the house, its urinals.

Nearly 5 feet in height and a yard wide, each floor-to-chest receptacle at first glance could have been mistaken for a porcelain sarcophagus. It was not a feature to be advertised, but one local paper named it the best urinal in Portland, according to original brewmaster Karl Ockert, who also remembered men sneaking their female companions into the men's room for a look.

"I always told people it was sort of a DUI indicator," he said. "Because if you couldn't hit that urinal, you'd had too much."

36

Creativity Pays

FOR SOME, CREATIVITY IN PORTLAND meant expressing yourself in any number of artistic, provocative, and sometimes off-beat ways. For others, it was a living,

Steve Sandstrom studied fine arts at the University of Oregon and made a name for himself drawing a comic strip for the student-run *Oregon Daily Emerald.* By creating a witty duck that came to rival the school's official mascot in popularity, Sandstrom won the Society of Professional Journalists' national Mark of Excellence Award for editorial cartooning.

Still, he realized he wasn't going to be Garry Trudeau and make a living off creating comic strips. He also gauged that he wouldn't make a living as an artist in Portland.

At one point, Sandstrom just wanted to get backstage. That was his motivation for entering a design contest sponsored by Portland radio station KGON, which invited listeners to create a valentine for the rock group Heart. The prize was a backstage pass for the upcoming concert featuring Heart and Little River Band. Sandstrom won, and when he came in second in a subsequent contest to design a T-shirt, KGON enlisted him for actual paying projects. One of the first, a new logo for the radio station, stuck quite literally.

"There were 500,000 bumper stickers on the streets of Portland," he said. "Every teenage kid had it plastered everywhere and it was on every cash register at every record store. It was all over the place."

His work for KGON eventually caught the eye of Peter Moore, Nike's creative director, who hired Sandstrom to create sales materials and graphics for Nike's apparel division. When Nike marketing head Rob Strasser left in 1986, Moore followed. Sandstrom wasn't far behind, as he set out to build his own design firm, first by partnering with ad agency Borders, Perrin & Norrander.

"That was in the late-'80s. It was a renaissance for me, because it just opened me up to the world of advertising," he said. "It was really smart, copy-driven stuff. Even if it was for a bank, or PGE or whatever, we would have a blast. It was out of the mold. It was just not traditional."

Sandstrom's agency became known for its brand identity work and innovative packaging for national brands such as Levi's, Coca-Cola, and Microsoft. But his most significant project was on behalf of a Portland-based company hoping to make tea the next big thing.

Portlander Steve Smith came to Sandstrom for help with his new company, explaining that tea was more than

7,000 years old, was consumed in various blends around the world, and that the vibe he wanted to create was "Marco Polo meets Merlin." He was crushed that his preferred name, Elixir, was taken.

"It was right at a time when people might consider acupuncture, maybe they'd consider Chinese herbs, maybe they'd consider doing yoga or meditation," Sandstrom said. "Traditional medicine was getting questioned. And so you have this alternative lifestyle starting to become more mainstream, and it was just like hitting the rapids at the right point. That's what happened."

Writer Steve Sandoz came up with the name: Tazo. Sandstrom developed the look. The vibe was mystical and new age. The list of ingredients, approved by the U.S. Food and Drug Administration, included "the mumbled chantings of a certified tea shaman." The logo featured a small 't' that looked like a cross and an 'o' with another cross that resembled a telescope sight. Think about an exploration on the high seas in Asia.

"We made it look like nothing that anybody had ever seen," Sandstrom said. "I thought it was going to be (perceived as) devil worship. I thought we were going to get hate mail. But the opposite actually happened. It just helped me learn, being brave and confident are pretty good traits to have."

Tazo launched in 1994 and whistled proudly from the start. Five years later Smith sold the company to Starbucks and in 2009 he started the Steven Smith Teamaker company, also with Sandstrom's support. When Smith died in 2015, the *New York Times* said he "helped transform the na-

Sandstrom Design provided Portland's Tazo Tea with instant brand recognition. (Photo courtesy of Sandstrom Partners)

tion's tea-drinking habits as much as any American since that party in Boston Harbor in 1773."

By the mid-1990s, creative agencies were popping up around Portland. Sasquatch Advertising, started by four former employees of Borders, Perrin & Norrander, opened in 1995 and quickly landed Portland-based Leatherman Tool Group as a client.

"The fact that we were based in Portland at that point was an advantage for us, just because we were already becoming kind of a creative hotbed," said Sasquatch co-founder Ken Chitwood. "Wieden had a reputation. Borders had a reputation. It was kind of pulling the rest of the city along."

That also meant more work for businesses that supported brands and agencies.

Downstream was a post-production house specializing in video and sound editing for commercials, video, and music projects, drawing work locally as well as nationally. The company spun off Tyee Productions, which shifted its focus to creating infomercials.

"It felt like we were turning into a major market, but we never thought about it that way," said Rick Waritz, a music producer and manager who transitioned to sound editing. "Downstream was kind of a hub for it, because we had the best gear, the best editors, the best sound designers. It's kind of just where everybody ended up for a period. So all the agency people were there. Nike was doing their stuff there. Adidas was growing and doing their stuff there. We had to be really careful if Nike and Adidas were in the shop at the same time. And Tyee was filling the house with infomercials and work for national firms. We were doing a lot of Wieden's work back in those days. So it was a real hub."

If creating content and other business-based creativity wasn't already lucrative enough in Portland, the Internet happened. From start-up online ventures, to brand websites, and interactive CD-ROM development, Portland entered a new world of opportunity.

"One thing that happened in the talent space is that anyone who could code any level of HTML was just immediately worth their weight in gold," said Steve Potestio, a longtime Portland creative recruiter. "Everyone was fighting over any level of talent that knew anything as it pertained to the Internet."

Portland was home to online businesses such as electronics online retailer 800.com and, briefly, wine.com. Interactive agencies, seeking to offer strategy, design, and production, included Pop Art, Cybersight, White Horse Interactive, and Paris France. Some established companies like Nike and Wieden+Kennedy created their own interactive departments.

And guess what? People were coming to Portland to join in.

"It created the opportunity for digital agencies or for the traditional agencies to expand into this digital realm," Potestio said. "And it continued to draw people to Portland, because Portland was starting to be seen as a place you could go where there was opportunity."

For many, opportunity had long been part of the Portland ethos, whether it was art, music, design, or anything to do with the Internet.

"Everybody was exploring something," Waritz said. "Portland was always, 'Oh, I'll go start a club, or I'll do a concert in the park.' You always just felt like it was a thing you could do. You could do anything and start it up. And if you got a couple more people together, they'd want to do it too, and it might turn into something. I don't know why the town engendered that kind of approach, but it always did."

37

More Brewers Pour In

BEGINNING IN 1985, PORTLAND ENJOYED a healthy taste of the new phenomenon known as brewpubs, with early brewers McMenamins, Bridgeport, Widmer Brothers, and Portland Brewing establishing a successful marketplace. In the early '90s, the city was ready for another round.

But not everyone agreed, as Gary Geist learned when he wrote a business plan for what would become the Lucky Labrador.

"We took that business plan out on the road to family, friends, friends of friends, just anybody who would listen to us," Geist said. "The number one question we got was, 'Don't you think there's enough breweries in Portland already?'"

Geist and his business partner, Alex Stiles, pressed on. The two boyhood friends from Lincoln High were working at Bridgeport, Stiles as a brewer and Geist as a bartender, and doing home brewing on the side. They eventually put their long talked-about plan into action, and, with the help of a small business administration loan, bought the former home of a sheet metal and roofing company on busy Southeast Hawthorne Boulevard.

Relying on several of their home brewing recipes, they opened the Lucky Lab in 1994. With an approach inspired by the original Bridgeport — simple food and counter service in an industrial atmosphere — the Lab kept the focus on draft beer sold only on the premises, staying away from the risk and expense of bottling and distribution. There weren't even TVs.

"It's sort of the English pub style, where people come here and there's nothing to do but converse," Geist said. A dog-friendly outdoor seating area was fitting, considering the name of the pub.

Second-generation breweries and pubs were sprouting up throughout Portland. Hair of the Dog began brewing in Southeast Portland. Tugboat Brewing was downtown, just off Southwest Broadway. The Old Lompoc poured on Northwest 23rd, the Old Market Pub welcomed customers on Portland's western edge in Garden Home, and the Alameda Brewhouse came to Northeast.

More brewpubs spawned more events to help publicize them. Beer drinkers could seek out their favorites at the Spring Beer Fest, held first at Multnomah Greyhound Park before moving to the Portland Expo Center. They could stay warm in a tent at the annual Holiday Ale Festival in Pioneer Courthouse Square. And they could get their chicken dance on at Oktoberfest in Oaks Park.

Of course, July brought the massive Oregon Brewers Festival, and smaller celebrations highlighted the warm summer months.

The passion for craft beer was not only recreational, but educational. Budding home brewers could take how-to courses on the subject at Portland Community College. Or beer fans could attend a series of Saturday lectures on microbrew culture at five Portland breweries and tour Oregon hop fields.

The Portland beer industry experienced a hiccup in the late-'90s. The Blitz-Weinhard Brewery, located at Northwest 12th and Burnside since 1864, closed in 1999. Of the earliest craft brewers, Bridgeport had changed ownership, Portland Brewing was rescued by investor Mac MacTarnahan, and Anheuser-Busch purchased more than a quarter-interest of Widmer Brothers. Second-generation brewer Nor'Wester collapsed and was purchased by Lake Oswego-based Saxer, which in turn was bought by Portland Brewing.

It was hard to imagine a couple decades later, with Portland having more than 100 breweries and brewpubs in the metro area, but in 1997 Saxer owner Steve Goebel painted an ominous picture of the future.

"Anybody who wants to get in the business in Oregon has missed the bus," Goebel told *The Oregonian*. "The bus pulled out a long time ago."

It didn't take long for the bus to come back, because Portland recovered, and the industry continued to grow. With the benefit of three decades of perspective, Lucky Lab's Geist has seen the market's staying power.

"I've just kind of noticed a general trend that once the economy kind of takes a downturn, there's always new breweries that come out of it," he said.

And that's what happened near the end of the decade. Over the next few years, soon-to-be favorites Laurelwood Brewing opened in the Hollywood District and Amnesia Brewing launched on North Mississippi Street. Portland Brewing co-founder Art Larrance opened the Raccoon Lodge in nearby Beaverton. Lompoc Brewing and the Lucky Lab added new locations and McMenamins continued to expand. Portland's thirst for craft beer only intensified.

Many have tried to analyze why Portland became Beervana. Certainly, the Northwest's fresh water and abundance of hops were essential to its beer industry. And maybe it was the rain that sent people inside to pubs, or the long summer nights that kept patios busy. Certainly a willingness to try new things helped the more adventurous brewers find an audience.

Not to be overlooked was the nature of the product itself. Alan Sprints, founder of Hair of the Dog Brewing, made it sound simple as he reflected back.

"I never liked that full feeling of too much beer," he told *The Oregonian.* "So when I started drinking beer, I gravitated toward stronger beer, beers you could have one or two of but get the same feeling as if you have six. So when I thought about opening a brewery, I thought if I made those ... that I'd have a place."

That place was Portland.

And another thing...

There were plenty of crafty promotions by craft brewers in the 1990s, but one went to the dogs. For the Lucky Labrador's first anniversary, co-owners Gary Geist and Alex Stiles placed a quarter-page ad in Willamette Week announcing a free dog wash on their patio. On the day of the event, enthusiasm was unleashed.

"We went out there at 11 o'clock, and there were already like 15 dogs lining up," Geist said. "Alex and I ended up washing 60 dogs that day."

After the successful first wash, Lucky Lab asked for small donations and turned the event into fundraiser for DoveLewis Emergency Animal Hospital.

"So the next year was about 150 dogs, and then it was 250 dogs," Geist said. "I think our high-water mark was about 650 dogs. And a horse. It was just mayhem."

The event has evolved into the annual Dogtoberfest street fair for DoveLewis at the Southeast Hawthorne location.

"We've got this awesome relationship with them and we've done a lot of fundraising for them," Geist said. "At the same time, I think they brought us a lot of business long term."

······ **38** ······

Reuse, Remake, and Refill

BY THE MID-1990S, MIKE AND Brian McMenamin had converted a poor farm to a hotel, a union hall to a theater, and a love for beer into more than 40 establishments in neighborhoods throughout the Northwest.

But with the Kennedy School, the brothers were graduating to something new altogether. For the first time, the McMenamins' ideas faced competition.

An elementary school that served the Concordia neighborhood for 60 years before closing in 1975, the Kennedy School was an abandoned eyesore when the city of Portland opened a proposal process to keep the Mediterranean-style building from demolition. Proposals to the Portland Development Commission (PDC) included a rest home and an indoor soccer facility, as well as the McMenamins' pitch for a pub-and-hotel complex.

"We had to go to a lot of meetings to try to explain ourselves, because the people hear there's a tavern going into the neighborhood and all they can think of is strippers and a bunch of drunk guys," Brian McMenamin said.

At the same time, the chain was so well established that the proposal drew a mostly positive response, especially when the McMenamins agreed to provide meeting space and a shared garden for the local community. The McMenamins, who grew up nearby, won out.

"(The PDC) really wanted us in that neighborhood to help the community," Brian McMenamin said. "That's the message we'd been trying to send for years. Somebody was buying it now."

Local officials, including Mayor Vera Katz, attended the opening ceremony in October 1997.

"It still sends a shiver down my spine," Brian said. "I was coming down 33rd (Avenue) and I was running late. All the news crews were set up with their satellite dishes and stuff. I thought, 'Boy, this is different. We got the key to the neighborhood.' And that's where it really stepped up."

At the time, Mike McMenamin called it "the granddaddy of all experiments."

The Kennedy School was a textbook example of what architects call adaptive reuse. Classrooms became hotel rooms or bars. The gym turned into a meeting room or reception hall. The auditorium was transformed into a theater, with couches and easy chairs. McMenamins' team of artists were allowed to run free, producing paintings reflective of the building's past. Ornate borders and retro fixtures added to the unique vibe of what became an escape in the middle of the city.

"It's so different than what you envisioned. How it ends up, it's just magical," Mike McMenamin said in video produced for the pub's 25th anniversary.

It was the best example of one of the things the McMenamins became best known for: renovating dying buildings with wild imagination and creativity.

"I love how they generally treat those buildings like found art," said Brad Cloepfil, an award-winning Portland architect. "There's something so incredibly, authentically Portland about it. I'm totally for just using what you have, but also doing it in such a cool, extreme way."

The same year the McMenamins gave a neighborhood elementary school new life, they did the same for an aging dance hall downtown. The Crystal Ballroom, which opened in 1914 as Ringler's Cotillion Hall, ceased operations as a concert hall in the 1960s. But with a $3 million renovation and seismic upgrade, the venue became one of the most successful concert halls in town. Ringler's Pub on the ground floor and Lola's Room, a smaller music outlet on the second floor, helped bring the Crystal Ballroom back to life in a big way.

Within the Crystal's first few years, The Presidents of the United States of America, Joan Jett & the Blackhearts, and Sleater-Kinney performed, as well as dozens of other local and national acts. Audiences bounced on the rejuvenated dance floor, which because of its system of rollers and rockers underneath, gave it a spring-like effect.

With the building's grand chandeliers, the design was about preserving — or re-creating — what had come before, including murals that nodded to the Crystal's history to go along with old rock posters from the '60s. Mike McMenamin described it as a combination of Venice meets Haight-Ashbury.

The structural engineer on the project, who also worked on the McMenamins' huge overhaul of Edgefield early in the decade, called out one of the qualities that made so many of the chain's establishments endearing and enduring.

"It's a pleasure to work with Mike because he saves things — sometimes the funkier, the better," Jerry Estroup told *The Oregonian*. "As an engineer, you tend to think that new is best, but he's starting to sway me to his way of thinking."

A generation later, the approach continues to impress, as McMenamins boasts 12 hotels and 64 restaurants, pubs, and bars, all with their creative, funky vibe.

"It's definitely its own genre," Cloepfil said. "You can renovate any old building and turn it into offices or condos or whatever you want to do. But the way they did stuff is like nothing else."

To some, McMenamins' frequent preservation and transformation of what otherwise might be forgotten buildings takes on a uniquely Portland flavor. Exploring a former farmhouse, a retirement home, or even a funeral chapel makes having a beer and a burger a borderline noble enterprise.

"Where else but Portland would someone have the creativity and the frame of mind to say, 'Hey, I got an idea: Let's go buy old churches or schools and transform them into restaurants and sort of entertainment centers,'" said former Nike ad director Scott Bedbury. "I would put McMenamins up there with that spirit of creativity that kind of defined Portland during that period."

Cheers to that.

···· **39** ····

What a Ride

TINKER HATFIELD USED TO RIDE his motor scooter to work from Southeast Portland to Nike's offices in Beaverton, crossing the Sellwood Bridge and navigating the streets through Southwest neighborhoods. He had no idea it would put him on a roller coaster that would land his creations in the Smithsonian Institution and his name on *Fortune*'s list of the top 100 designers of the 20th century. By 1999, he needed to get off the ride.

All Hatfield had done over the previous dozen years was uncover Nike's greatest technology for the world to see, launch an entire new category of shoes, form the greatest athlete-designer partnership in history, and — according to company co-founder Phil Knight — save Nike. And that was just part of his workload.

After playing a key creative role in the company's annual growth from approximately $1 billion to around $9 billion, Hatfield needed to get away from it all. So he and his wife traveled — to Miami, the Caribbean, Europe, New York, and the countryside.

"We ended up back in Portland and I made an observation," he said. "I was unable to go anywhere in the world and not see something that I personally had designed."

Get away, yes. From it all, no.

That there was always something there to remind him was testament of Hatfield's journey from three-sport star in high school, to college pole vaulter at the University of Oregon, to Nike corporate architect, to being widely acknowledged as the greatest sneaker designer in history. Starting at Nike in 1981, his duties included designing office space and showrooms at a time the company's product designs were growing stale. In 1985, marketing vice president Rob Strasser and creative director Peter Moore called for an internal design contest.

"You had 24 hours," Hatfield recalled of the assignment. "There were about 14 footwear designers at the time and then they threw in a couple other people, including myself. I worked all 24 hours."

Hatfield designed a shoe built for riding a motor scooter but suitable for walking around. His elaborate presentation resulted in his immediate reassignment to the position of shoe designer at twice his salary. It also previewed where Hatfield would lead the entire sneaker industry, with designs made for technical performance but with a fashionable appearance.

The first shoe Hatfield designed for Nike in 1986 is one of his most famous — the Air Max running shoe. Inspired by Paris' Centre Pompidou and its ventilation, heating, and water systems on the outside, Hatfield designed a shoe that showed previously hidden Nike Air technology through an opening in the heel. In the same year, he designed the Air Trainer, the first cross-training shoe and Nike's response to Reebok's market rise through aerobics.

Hatfield's next design, the Air Jordan 3, might have been his most important. Strasser and Moore had left Nike to start their own company and Michael Jordan was considering following them. After seeing Hatfield's design, Jordan ultimately decided to stay. The Jordan 3, backed by Wieden+Kennedy's advertising campaign pairing Jordan and Spike Lee, proved hugely successful, helping to launch Nike into a new era of prosperity.

It also started a run of Hatfield-Jordan collaborations that usually were celebrated as the biggest release in the industry each year. Hatfield became close with Jordan as they worked toward the next model.

"I was basically staying in his house virtually any time of the year," Hatfield said. "I'd ask him some questions on the phone and he'd say, 'I can't answer it, because I'll have to think about it. Once you come out and just stay for three or four or five days, we'll figure it out.' He put everybody on notice that he was trying to be the best ever, and he wanted his shoes to be the best ever, and to be unique and be fashion and trendsetting along with satisfying his needs as a player."

Air Jordans elevated style and contributed mightily to shoe brands' connection to hip-hop culture. By the mid-

1990s, sneakers were broadly accepted as everyday wear, even in one of the fashion capitals of the world.

"It was coming of age, this particular part of design," Hatfield said. "For the first 10 years that Nike was cool, we were struggling to kind of get things rolling in Paris and parts of Europe. It finally kind of broke open and it became cool to wear sneakers with whatever else you were wearing."

The zenith came with the Air Jordan 11. Jordan had retired from the NBA in 1993 — for all anyone knew it was forever — and there were those at Nike who thought the Air Jordan series should be retired with him. Hatfield argued against it and created what he has said was his all-time favorite, a classic white shoe rimmed in shiny, black patent leather.

"I put everything that I could think of into that shoe," Hatfield said. He had a brief time window to show the sample to Jordan, who was playing minor-league baseball, so he presented the shoe in the clubhouse of the ballpark in Birmingham, Alabama.

More than a quarter-century later, Hatfield still remembers Jordan's reaction.

"The first thing he said is 'People are going to get married in these things ... this is like the first basketball shoe you could wear with a tuxedo or a suit.' I said, 'Wow, that's not what I was shooting for, but if you say so.' Sure enough, a few months later Boyz II Men wore them with tuxedos to the Grammys. He called me right up and said, 'I told you so.'"

Jordan returned to basketball and wore the Jordan 11 to win his fourth NBA championship in 1996, the same year the movie *Space Jam* was released with Jordan wearing an all-black version of the shoe.

By then, Nike had contributed greatly to Portland's population increase in the '90s, infusing the area with young, creative people from far and wide.

"Nike was now attracting people from New York City and Los Angeles, Berlin and London. They were coming here because they knew about Nike, but they also now knew about Oregon or Portland," Hatfield said. "They kind of demanded that there would be better restaurants and hipper, cooler places to hang out. So it's not all about just the beauty of the natural environment, it's also, 'What's cool in Portland?'"

For Hatfield, there was plenty. With more than a decade of global travel under his belt, he saw how Portland measured up.

"I was actually more aware than a lot of folks that Portland was turning this corner and it was becoming a city of the world, not just the Pacific Northwest," he said. "And I thought that was very cool."

40

Pearl 4: An Expanded Vision

HE'S BEEN CALLED A VISIONARY many times over. To see what Homer Williams envisioned in Portland's Pearl District, go to Northwest 11th Avenue between Irving and Johnson Streets and look north.

There, as far as the eye can see, stand multi-story condominium buildings with a steady procession of retail shops, salons, coffee outposts, and the like on ground floors. Walk north and you'll also see urban parks, on a good day filled with parents and their young children, workers on a break, people enjoying the sun, and a representative share of the homeless population.

A generation ago, the spot you'd be standing on was the site of a contaminated rail yard. Then Williams, whose Hoyt Street Properties owned the land, got to work doing what he does best.

"We all have different gifts. I'm pretty good about seeing into the future, and I always have been," said Williams, an admitted demographics freak. "I couldn't build a box, but I can tell you what I think ought to happen, and I've always been able to kind of forge ahead."

Williams was not alone in seeing the potential for what was believed to be the largest parcel of vacant land near an urban core in the country, land which would eventually become a huge part of the Pearl. You can see it in the River District Development Plan, referring to what the area was known as before the Pearl. The product of a 10-person steering committee, city departments, neighborhood associations, and others, it provided "a Development Plan for Portland's North Downtown" in 1994. The conclusion of the 41-page report called back to the earliest days of Portland's renaissance, with the same optimism:

"Portland has demonstrated repeatedly during the last two decades an ability to redevelop parts of its Central City in a more predictable fashion than other cities. It has removed a freeway and built a riverfront park. It has rebuilt downtown streets as high-capacity transit streets. It has constructed a convention center. It has and continues to build a successful light rail system. All of these projects have stimulated construction of private and public development ten to fifty times the cost of the original public investment. Although virtually all other major U.S. cities have pursued similar projects, none has implemented as many as Portland."

The report went on to say, "But, if it does happen can it be wonderful? It seems so. Portland is a prudent, practical place where frequently something wonderful does happen. The River District aspires to be that kind of place, nothing more."

The report called out what many already knew. The area presented a golden opportunity to expand what already was happening in the Pearl District, including to the west on Northwest 13th Avenue with Al Solheim's Irving Street Lofts and John Carroll's Chown Pella Lofts.

"What was cool about it, it felt very organic," writer Randy Gragg said of the evolution of the Pearl. "It had all these different people doing all these different projects, and it all just kind of popped up and came together."

As Williams said, "There's so many fingerprints on the Pearl."

When Pat Prendergast bought out Carroll's share of the 40-acre Burlington Northern rail yards, Williams came on as the managing partner of Hoyt Street Properties, putting him in a position to leave one of the largest fingerprints on the area. It helped that government officials were aggressively pro-development.

"Everybody kind of had to make deals together," Gragg said. "Vera was exceptionally good at that."

Vera Katz, Portland's mayor from 1993-2005, led Portland during a time of advancements in urban living and the revitalization of its neighborhoods. Like Mayor Neil Goldschmidt in the 1970s, Katz was known as someone who made things happen.

"Neil ruled by power, and Vera ruled by deal-making," Gragg said.

As a girl, Katz left Germany for France with her family shortly after Hitler came into power. When the Nazis invaded

France, the family escaped on foot to Spain and eventually moved to the U.S. After growing up in Brooklyn, Vera and her then-husband, artist Mel Katz, moved to Portland in 1964. She entered politics after being inspired by Robert Kennedy's 1968 presidential campaign and was elected to Oregon's House of Representatives in 1972, and in 1985 became Oregon's first woman speaker of the house. As Portland's mayor, her energy and optimism mirrored the city's.

"She loved the city," Gragg said. "She'd make you go walk with her. She was an introvert, but when she was out and people would come up to her, you'd just watch her turn it on."

It certainly didn't hurt that Katz was a fan of Williams and his vision for development in Portland. "Homer is unique," Katz told *Willamette Week* in 2003. "He sees possibilities other people don't see."

That view was no doubt shaped by Williams' efforts in the Pearl and, before that, Forest Heights, a housing development deal he cobbled together west of downtown. In the process, Williams developed a reputation for collaboration and perseverance.

"Homer is a humble guy, and he's smart enough to realize he doesn't have all the answers," Michael Czysz, an architect on the Pearl District Neighborhood Association board, said in 1998.

It took a willingness to collaborate for Williams to move ahead in the Pearl. Working with willing partners on the Portland Development Commission, as well as neighborhood advocacy groups, negotiations included a series of tradeoffs by the city for increased levels of housing density.

The city agreed to tear down the Lovejoy Ramp, a roadway that connected Portland's Westside to the Broadway Bridge and the East side, but also split the proposed neighborhood in two. It pledged to support and invest in a streetcar line that would travel from the Northwest neighborhood to Portland State University in the Southwest downtown area. And it committed to building three new city parks, resulting in Jamison Square, Tanner Springs Park, and The Fields Park. In exchange, the commitment on the development side was to build 150 residential units per acre, creating the most densely populated neighborhood in Portland.

"The agreement, that one action, codified these two key events: the deal with the railroads, and the deal to get the Lovejoy ramp torn down and rebuilt," Bruce Allen, then-development manager for the PDC, said of the 1997 agreement. "You couldn't have done anything without those acres, and you couldn't have done much without tearing down that ramp."

In removing the ramp, Portland also lost a unique collection of art drawn on the 30-foot-concrete pillars supporting the structure. The chalk-and-paint artwork mixed Greek Mythology, Biblical imagery, and historic America and stood for 50 years. It was drawn by Tom Stefopoulos, a night watchman at the rail yard who frequently stood on top of boxcars to reach his canvas.

The Lovejoy Columns' star turn came in Gus Van Sant's 1989 movie, *Drugstore Cowboy*, which featured scenes with the lead characters underneath the ramp in the yet-to-be developed neighborhood. Today, two of the columns can be seen on Northwest 10th Avenue between Everett and Flanders at Carroll's Elizabeth Lofts building.

Williams' vision began to take shape in September 1998 with the completion of the Riverstone, a six-story, 123-unit condominium building featuring ground-floor retail at Northwest 11th between Johnson and Kearney. A block south and 18 months later, Johnson Street Townhomes opened. Offering 13 rowhouse units, each with its own garden space, it was named "Project of the Year" by *Builder Magazine*.

Steps away, Kearney Plaza, with 131 apartments, and Tanner Place condominiums and its 121 units, were completed in July 2001. The ground-floor retail opportunities in the buildings, as well as Portland's short, 200-foot blocks, were essential to the energy in the area

"It's 30 feet and below. If you get that right, you've got a neighborhood," Williams said. "If you don't get it right, you don't have a neighborhood. It is that simple."

Those first four Hoyt Street Properties projects, along with the 13-story Park Place condominiums built a few years later, surrounded the Pearl's first new park, Jamison Square. Named after the late gallery owner William Jamison, the park is best known for its fountain and the shallow pools of water that made it a perfect destination for young children on a hot day. For Williams, the unintended consequences were a delight to watch evolve.

"Nobody thought every mother in the West Hills was going to bring her kid down there," he said. "It changed the retail down there. The ice cream shop, clothes for kids, and things like that. You've just got to go with the flow."

Jamison Square, named after gallery owner William Jamison, opened in 2002.

By 2002, Williams had given up his interest in Hoyt Street Properties, which continued to build on the former rail yard property under the management of his stepdaughter Tiffany Sweitzer. To date, it has developed about a third of the more than 30 condo buildings in the Pearl. Williams turned his attention to large projects in downtown Los Angeles and another new neighborhood, Portland's South Waterfront District.

"He's an idea guy, and he really likes getting the ideas and going with it," said longtime Pearl District Realtor Debbie Thomas. "Homer had the vision and then let other people take over doing the implementing. But he's behind a ton of buildings, and a ton of ideas."

And those around the emerging Pearl District knew it. Shawn Levy, former film critic for *The Oregonian*, visited New York on the set of Van Sant's 2000 film, *Finding Forrester*. Van Sant asked Levy how things were in Portland and the two talked about the rapid changes in the Pearl.

"We were joking that they ought to name that district after Homer Williams," Levy said. "On my last day on the set, I said goodbye to Gus and he said, 'Tell Homer City hello for me.'"

And another thing...

It was 2002 and Homer Williams' phone rang. On the other end was Ray Nagin, the new mayor of New Orleans.

"Somebody told me I need to talk to you. I want to do what you did in Portland, Oregon," said Nagin, as explained by Williams.

"We talked. He's a very charming guy," Williams said. "And I said, 'Look, let me make it really simple. You need to send somebody out here, and you need to study the Portland Development Commission and what they do. If you do that, then you will begin to understand Portland.'"

As the conversation wound down, Williams had one more thing about New Orleans on his mind.

"I said, 'Ray, I've got to ask you a question. Are you still going to have all that graft? Because if you are, it won't work. (He said) Oh, no, no. I'm going to fix that.'"

In 2014, Nagin was found guilty on 20 corruption charges, including taking more than $500,000 in bribes in exchange for lucrative city contracts. He was sentenced to 10 years in federal prison.

41

One Call Changed It All

IT WAS A NIGHT THAT Brad Cloepfil will never forget. It was 1996 and two years of struggling to build his own architecture firm into a success while trying to pay a mortgage and support a wife and three children was coming to a head. As with many couples, financial challenges brought stress into the open.

"We got into this huge fight," Cloepfil recalled. "She said, 'You know, you're only making like $17,000 a year. You're almost 40 years old. Maybe you should get a real job.'"

Cloepfil left the house and went to his office, contemplating the future of his business and his marriage. His only prospect for meaningful work, a new head-quarters building for Portland's preeminent ad agency, Wieden+Kennedy, was mired in a competitive process with multiple firms.

"I was barely in business. I was starving to death," he said. "So I was dying (waiting for an answer), because I knew it would change my entire life."

When he got to his office on that pivotal night, Cloepfil noticed a message on his office phone's answering machine. With so much riding on the outcome, the voice revealed little.

"This is Wieden. Call me."

Who needs a drink?

"So I'm like shaking, shaking, shaking, shaking," Cloepfil said. "I can't take it. I went to the bar next door, Crackerjacks, and I had a scotch."

Earlier that evening, Dan Wieden called Kristy Edmunds, whose Portland Institute of Contemporary Art would find a home in W+K's eventual new headquarters. The agency's leadership was split on a decision between Cloepfil's Allied Works and the much larger, more-established Boora Architects. Wieden would make the final decision and wanted to know what Edmunds thought. It's hard to know if the conversation swayed Wieden's decision or confirmed it.

"What I said was if you want to hearken back to the beginning, when Phil Knight took a chance on you as a young start-up, then you would go with Allied," she said. "And if you want to work with your peers at the level that you have now achieved, you would go with Boora."

Suitably bolstered from his detour to Crackerjacks, Cloepfil went back to his office and returned Wieden's call. The job was his.

That Cloepfil had even been in the running came about from his work on Bruce Carey's shiny new restaurant,

Saucebox, which had opened the previous year. When Susan Hoffman, a W+K creative director, asked the bartender who designed the space, it led to Cloepfil's months-long journey that included at least three interviews with Wieden. In one meeting, Cloepfil, teaching a class at University of Oregon at the time, filled his office with students to make it look like he had more than his actual two employees.

Once Cloepfil got the assignment, the search began for the site of what would become Portland's last great architectural success story of the 20th century. It would have to replace the existing reality of Wieden+Kennedy employees working in eight different buildings in town. They considered buildings in Northwest and the Eastside, but the best candidate was on Northwest 13th Avenue between Davis and Everett. The 90-year-old building started as the Fuller Paint Company and was last used as a cold-storage facility before languishing in disrepair.

"That was the only building that was really big enough for them to hold something like 450 people," Cloepfil said. "Dan looked at it and said 'Nope,' because all the windows were all bricked in and it was pitch black. You know, it was not very happy. I said, 'Just let me show you what it could be.'"

The audacity of the project and the plans stirred anticipation. Pat Harrington, a partner at Boora Architects and a boardmember at PICA, called it an "extraordinary example of adaptive re-use."

"Wieden+Kennedy will be transforming a building most people would find completely unappealing into a major catalyst for the district," he said in 1997.

*Before and after. Allied Works turned a cold storage building into Wieden+
Kennedy headquarters. (Photos courtesy of Allied Works Architecture)*

The result was a stunning do-over of a 22,000-square-
foot space, a five-story atrium "building within a building"
with a central, open theater space featuring rows of bleach-
ers that allowed the whole company to gather. By the time
the building opened in 2000, the total cost was a reported
$36 million.

To Wieden, it was worth it.

"If you have a chance to do something like this, you've
got to go for it," he told *The Oregonian*. "Ads are so dispos-
able: ink on paper or light coming through the air. With a
building, you're leaving tracks for a long time."

The Wieden+Kennedy building encompassed many of
the elements of Portland's renaissance: creativity, art, architecture and even dining when Bluehour, the building's
street-level, corner restaurant opened. The agency's headquarters was the crown jewel of Portland's fast-emerg-
ing Pearl District, with W+K's hundreds of employees and
their clients securing the neighborhood's reputation as
Portland's creative nerve center.

"For us, this wasn't about the riddle of figuring out the cubicles or making the office space different than the next guy's," Wieden said at the time. "The job was figuring out how we can help people live creative lives. I don't care whether you're a writer or in finance or simply coming to visit us. If we're helping people lead surprising, audacious lives, that will infect everything else we do here."

It was just part of the reason Wieden welcomed PICA rent free for three years. Edmunds' brainchild, with its focus on promoting emerging, contemporary artists, gave the Pearl yet another energy source for art in an 8,000-foot space that included a 2,200-square-foot-gallery. Wieden, who once tried to hire Edmunds, wanted it nearby.

The inclusion of Bluehour, Carey's upscale replacement for Zefiro, confirmed that the Pearl had become the next cool place to be.

"Portland is really ready for a swank dining room," Carey told *The Oregonian,* adding that its design was meant to be "soft and pretty," a contrast as the most-visible space of the industrial building.

Working on a shoestring budget for previous creations Zefiro and Saucebox, Carey was thrilled to have Wieden as a backer on Bluehour.

"Opening Bluehour was so much fun, between us just having a comfortable budget, and I really got to exercise my interest in interior design," Carey said. "Working with Brad was very collaborative, and to have it well received was great."

From Cloepfil's perspective, Carey brought a lot to the party.

"Bruce is so good, he could have done it himself. Just a natural architect," he said. "And it became a pretty cool place. It was aspiring to take its place with these other major West Coast cities."

At the same time, Clopefil's Allied Works was taking its place among the more creative architecture firms in the country. In the decade after the award-winning Wieden+Kennedy building was finished, Allied's projects included the Contemporary Art Museum in St. Louis, the 16-story building that houses the Seattle Art Museum, a major update of New York's Museum of Art and Design, the expansion of Booker T. Washington High School for the Performing & Visual Arts in Dallas, and a $42 million expansion of the University of Michigan Museum of Art.

And it all comes back to one anxiety-ridden night that changed everything for Cloepfil. He still marvels at Wieden's willingness to take a chance on him.

"He was the most amazing man," Cloepfil said shortly after Wieden's death in 2022. "I mean, how many thousands of people owe their careers and their view of work and everything to him. It was like he walked through a door and your life is entirely different. That's what happened with that phone call."

That was the lesson of Portland's renaissance. Over and over, people took chances, on starting a business, imagining an ad campaign, or investing in a new neighborhood. Or on opening a restaurant, or a gallery, or a pub. Or on conceiving new ways to bring people together, at an art walk, or a festival, or at a central square. With creativity as its guiding force, Portland was transformed.

Afterword
So, what's next?

On New Year's Eve in 1999, a crowd estimated as large as 50,000 ignored Y2K doomsday scenarios and gathered in and around Pioneer Courthouse Square to celebrate the arrival of the Year 2000. Rather than getting trapped on a MAX light rail train or dodging chaos in the streets, they listened to bands and watched a laser light show, once again fulfilling Will Martin's vision when he designed the square as "a downtown living room for the people of Portland."

In the years since its opening in 1984, the square had played host to hundreds, maybe thousands, of events, welcomed countless workers enjoying their lunch breaks, and served as a primary stop along the Max line beginning in 1986. As envisioned, it became a centralized hub to a revitalized downtown.

Two months earlier, Wieden+Kennedy had its own take on Y2K in a commercial for Nike. Directed by Spike Jonze and shot in Los Angeles, the spot showed multiple car crashes, crowds looting stores, money shooting out of ATMs, a wayward missile, and an escaped giraffe, all as a jogger ignores it while taking his daily run. "The Morning

After" won a 2000 Primetime Emmy Award for Outstanding Commercial, Wieden's first win in a category that was introduced three years earlier, no doubt to recognize the quality in television advertising that W+K helped advance.

Wieden+Kennedy continued to advance in the new century, maintaining eight offices around the world by 2010. Firmly putting to rest the notion that its success relied solely on Nike, the agency won the Primetime Emmy for Outstanding Commercial four years in a row from 2009-2012, for Coca-Cola, Old Spice, Chrysler, and Procter & Gamble. Today, the small firm that began with two men, a card table, and a pay phone in 1982 is the largest independent advertising agency in the world.

Other elements that drew attention to Portland continued to build.

With its roots in the '90s, the city's appetite for good, interesting dining continued to thrive in more interesting ways. The three owners of Zefiro split off — Bruce Carey to 23 Hoyt and Clarklewis, Chris Israel to Gruner, and Monique Siu to Castagna and then OK Omen. Other Zefiro alumni included Andy Ricker at Pok Pok and Vito Dilullo at Ciao Vito. Cathy Whims moved on from Genoa to open Nostrana, Gabriel Rucker worked at Paley's Place before opening Le Pigeon, and, three years after opening Beast, Naomi Pomeroy emerged as one of America's Top 10 Best New Chefs in *Food & Wine* magazine in 2009.

A generation after emerging as a forerunner of craft brewing, Portland could lay legitimate claim to being the best beer city in America. More local brewers offered more interesting beers to a draft-loving citizenry. Three out-of-town Oregon-based brewers, Rogue, Deschutes, and 10 Barrel, all moved into the Pearl District. Even a hipster-led movement toward lighter, cheaper Pabst Blue Ribbon could not slow the flow. By 2016, according to the Oregon Brewers Association, the Portland metro area was home to 105 breweries that contributed mightily to the nearly $5 billion annual economic impact of the beer industry statewide.

The Pearl District continued to expand in multiple directions, with high-rise condominiums to the north and the brewery blocks around the former Henry Weinhard brewery to the south. The Portland streetcar opened in 2001, formally connecting the former "scary warehouse district" to downtown and, eventually, the South Waterfront District.

Adidas scored a local public relations win when it left the suburbs and opened its new headquarters in a former Kaiser hospital building in North Portland in 2002. But Beaverton-based Nike, with more than $50 billion in earnings in 2023, has far outpaced its German rival in the global sneaker wars. Together, they remain prime attractions for young designers and marketers, as well as other athletic wear brands, to move to Portland.

Even Portland's first great ad campaign, "One Tough Mother" from Columbia Sportswear and Borders, Perrin & Norrander, survived into the 21st century and, after a 10-year gap, returned in 2015. A newer agency, North, handled the creative work, indicative of the evolving nature of Portland's advertising market. There were traditional agencies, small shops, and individual contractors all racing to keep up with new platforms.

Portland in the 21st century had long abandoned former Gov. Tom McCall's 1970s urging for people to visit Oregon "but for heaven's sake, don't come here to live." The annual population increases of the 1990s slowed, but Portland famously was still attracting young, educated people to a city that was affordable, healthy, and, yes, weird.

"It's really captured the zeitgeist of the age in a way that no other small city in America ever has," Aaron Renn, an urban-affairs analyst, told *The New York Times Magazine* in 2014. "People move to New York to be in media or finance; they move to L.A. to be in show business. People move to Portland to move to Portland."

And then 2020 happened. Nearly two months of nightly protests-turned-riots in the aftermath of George Floyd's killing in Minneapolis did extensive damage to downtown, as well as Portland's national reputation. The Covid pandemic and resulting work-from-home movement further hollowed the downtown core. Affordability has been an issue for years. Crime, open-air drug use, and widespread tent encampments have contributed to fears that Portland's best days are behind it.

Are they?

Many of the people I talked with for this book think so, citing the existing problems and doubtful that solutions can be found. Others remain hopeful, mindful that much of what allowed Portland to thrive still exists. A voter-approved revamp of city government in 2022 offers hope, and new efforts toward inclusivity are emerging.

I choose to look at it all with Rose City-colored glasses. The things that make Portland shine outweigh its blight.

Portland is still surrounded by the natural beauty and recreational opportunities of Mount Hood, the Oregon Coast, forests, parks, and rivers. It still has relatively mild weather, something that will become even more important as climate change continues, and its individual neighborhoods make for a city in constant change. Moreover, there's still a spirit of initiative and creativity that produces a steady stream of new opportunities to pursue and enjoy, from new restaurants and food carts, to neighborhood brewpubs, art shows, and businesses seeking creative talent.

Throughout the 1980s and '90s, people in Portland recognized challenges and seized opportunities to make life better for themselves and often for other Portlanders. They showed creativity in any number of ways and accepted it in others. It made for a vibrant, exciting, quirky city that residents took pride in and visitors envied.

It was a time of positivity and possibility. It was a renaissance. It will be up to a new generation to determine if it can happen again.

Epilogue
Where are they are now?

I'm grateful to all the people who offered their perspective on the story of Portland's renaissance. Here are life updates on many of the key figures who were featured in this book and remain active in Portland and beyond.

Former Nike advertising director **Scott Bedbury** was the chief marketing officer for Starbucks from 1995-98, during which time the coffee chain's annual revenues nearly tripled to more than $1.3 billion. Through his company Brandstream, he has advised well-known firms such as Airbnb, Kaiser Permanente, Coca-Cola and Microsoft. In 2002, he co-authored *A New Brand World: Ten Principles for Achieving Brand Leadership in the 21st Century*, and as of 2023 is working on a book about preserving trust and humanity in the disinformation age.

As a co-founder of Blackfish Gallery, **Barbara Black** has been displaying her paintings there for more than 40 years. When the artist-run cooperative moved after 36 years in the same Pearl District space, Black's art was part of the inaugural show at 938 Northwest Everett Street in late-2022.

Long after achieving popular and commercial success creating music videos in the 1980s, **Jim Blashfield** was still making animated short films and genre-challenging live action narratives well into the new century. Blashfield has also produced compelling public art installations, most recently "Mechanism" in Seattle and "Flooded Date Machine" on Portland's Tillikum Crossing. He was featured in the 2023 documentary, *History, Mystery & Odyssey: Six Portland Animators,* along with Joanna Priestley, Chel White, Rose Bond, Joan Gratz and Zak Margolis. Blashfield's partner and producer, **Melissa Marsland**, after directing for the theater and producing for various animators, recently retired from a 17-year teaching career. She is currently a substitute teacher for Portland Public Schools, an activist on local environmental issues, and has adapted six Mario Benedetti short stories for the stage.

Bill Borders co-founded one of Portland's most successful and creative ad agencies of the 1980s, Borders, Perrin & Norrander. To quote from his website, "Now I write books for kids, which is less profitable but *way* more rewarding." Borders lives in northern Idaho. His first children's book, *A Horn is Born,* was published in 2020. He also creates cartoons, screenplays and song lyrics, and yes, still dabbles in advertising.

Karen Brooks is Portland's defining veteran food voice, with tours of duty at *Willamette Week*, *The Oregonian*, and currently *Portland Monthly*. She has authored nine books on food and drink and in 2017 she received the prestigious James Beard Craig Claiborne Distinguished Restaurant Reviewer Award. In 2022, Brooks narrated episodes of Netflix's *Chef's*

Table: Pizza and *Street Foods: USA,* and in 2021 she guest-starred in Hulu's *Eater's Guide to the Universe.*

After starting Zefiro in 1990, Portland restaurateur **Bruce Carey** opened Saucebox, Bluehour and 23Hoyt, all of which enjoyed long runs before closing during Covid and its aftermath. He currently owns Clarklewis in Southeast Portland.

Since leaving Wieden+Kennedy in 1999, **Janet Champ** has continued her award-winning career as a freelance creative director and writer. Her clients have included Apple, Under Armour, Stand Up To Cancer, Chevy, and DocuSign. She concepted and wrote the Nike Foundation's 2014 Girl Effect Declaration, which was presented to the United Nations, and has co-authored two books, *Ripe* and *The Making of the Film: The Curious Case of Benjamin Button.*

Since the opening of the Wieden+Kennedy headquarters in Portland's Pearl District in 2000, **Brad Cloepfil** and his firm, Allied Works Architecture, have been in steady demand. Major projects in the last decade include the National Music Centre of Canada in Calgary and the National Veterans Memorial and Museum in Columbus, Ohio. Closer to home, Allied's finished projects can be seen at the Sokol Blosser Winery Tasting Room in Dayton, the Pacific Northwest College of Art, and the expanded Providence Park.

After starting and running the Portland Institute for Contemporary Art, **Kristy Edmunds** left Portland in 2005 to become the artistic director for the Melbourne International Art Festival. She was the executive and artistic director at UCLA's Center for the Art of Performance for 10 years before taking over as the director of the Massachusetts Museum of Contemporary Art in 2021.

Tinker Hatfield is vice president for design and special projects at Nike, where he has worked for more than 40 years creating many of the biggest-selling sneaker models of all time. In addition to public speaking, he still designs and mentors at Nike as well as devoting time to personal art projects.

Bob Hicks has covered art and culture in the Pacific Northwest since 1978, including for 25 years for *The Oregonian.* An author of several art books, he is also the executive editor of *Oregon Artswatch* (orartswatch.org).

Marty Hughley has been a journalist in Portland for more than 35 years, writing about pop music, theater, dance, and more. After working at *Willamette Week* and *The Oregonian*, Hughley is the theater editor for *Oregon Artswatch* (orartswatch.org). He was inducted to the Oregon Music Hall of Fame in 2013.

In 1994, along with co-owner Paul Mallory, **Greg Higgins** opened Higgins Restaurant, providing a stage for sustainable dining and a launching pad for a number of successful chefs in Portland. During the pandemic in 2020, Higgins opened Piggins, a food-cart bistro just outside the nearby Oregon Historical Society. The main restaurant continues to serve locally sourced and inspired dishes 30 years after opening.

Owner of the Augen Gallery since 1979 and one of the originators of the First Thursday art walk, **Bob Kochs** continues to offer limited-edition fine art prints from renowned artists including Frank Stella, Roy Lichtenstein and Andy Warhol. In 2007, Kochs opened a second space just outside the Pearl District in the DeSoto Building at 716 Northwest Davis, where he shows work from local and national artists.

A leader of Portland's contemporary arts scene for more than 40 years, **Elizabeth Leach** moved her gallery from the Old Town Historic District to the Pearl District at 417 Northwest 9th Avenue in 2004. She continues to participate in First Thursday and is an ardent supporter of the Portland art community. In 2016 she founded the Converge 45 Biennial, which features regional, national, and international artists in a citywide exhibition organized by a prominent guest curator.

A former film critic for *The Oregonian* and *KGW-TV*, **Shawn Levy** is a film historian, author, and passionate Portland Timbers fan. To date he has written 11 books, including biographies of Robert DeNiro, Paul Newman, and Jerry Lewis.

Forty years after opening their first pub together, **Mike and Brian McMenamin** are still building for the future, even with 56 properties in Oregon and Washington. Current or soon-to-be projects include expanding the property in Kalama, Washington, adding lodging at the Cornelius Pass Roadhouse in Hillsboro, and converting the former county jail into lodging and services at Edgefield in Troutdale.

Karl Ockert, the brewmaster when Bridgeport Brewing opened in 1984, has remained in the beer industry and worked at multiple breweries in and out of Portland, including Deschutes Brewery in Bend, Oregon, from 2015–2018. He is currently an industry consultant, educator, and author, and is working on his next book, *The Craft Brewer's Guide to Best Practices.*

A longtime recruiter of creative talent in Portland, **Steve Potestio** opened Harvester Talent in 2023. The agency matches those in creative fields such as design, marketing, and digital platforms with employers for temporary and permanent roles.

In the 1980s and '90s, **Jim Riswold** created some of the advertising industry's most memorable campaigns for Wieden+Kennedy. Since then, health issues led him to leave advertising and take up art. His 2017 memoir *Hitler Saved My Life* draws from his exhibitions showing figurines of historical villains placed in ridiculous settings and hilariously details his battles with leukemia and prostate cancer. Really. More recently Riswold has taken on the role of "grand influencer" at Wieden+Kennedy.

A visual artist for 50 years, **Tad Savinar** also has worked as an urban planner and served on the City of Portland Design Commission. He has created public art throughout Portland and served as a design team member on the Westside Light Rail project, the Oregon Holocaust Memorial in Washington Park, and others. His most recent visual arts exhibition, "Musings From the Future," at PDX Contemporary Gallery in January 2023, addressed civic and cultural conditions within the country.

Steve Sandstrom is the founder of Sandstrom Design, now Sandstrom Partners, which specializes in branding and development work, including identity, packaging, and design in the physical and digital worlds. He has won numerous design awards, including from The One Show,

Communication Arts, the Clio Awards, and the London International Advertising Awards.

After opening and running Wildwood restaurant from 1994 to 2007, chef **Cory Schreiber** taught culinary arts and chef training at the Art Institute of Portland for nearly seven years. A longtime proponent of local food sourcing, Schreiber is now a chef consultant for Sysco, advising the nation's largest foodservice marketer and producer on efficiencies while maintaining quality.

Often called "The Father of the Pearl District," developer **Al Solheim** remains active in his business and community involvement. Solheim was an early supporter of the Portland Institute for Contemporary Art and served on its board of directors. He also spent more than 20 years on the board of the Pacific Northwest College of Art, where he was awarded an honorary doctorate of arts. He currently serves on the board of the Northwest Community Conservancy, which works to improve conditions in the Pearl District.

More than 30 years after opening her real estate brokerage in Portland, **Debbie Thomas** maintains her office on the ground floor of the Chown Pella Lofts building. Serving commercial and residential clients, her company focuses on the Pearl District and other high-density neighborhoods.

Gordon Thompson, the creative director behind the original Niketown store in Portland, was Nike's global creative director for footwear, apparel and image from 1996-2002. He moved to Nike-owned Cole-Haan in 2002 and introduced Nike Air cushioning to fashion footwear, earning multiple guest appearances on "The Oprah Winfrey

Show." He has worked as an independent creative consultant since 2007 and lives in New York City.

In the 1980s and '90s, **Rick Waritz** was a band manager, a music producer, and a sound engineer. He is now the Vice President of Strategic Accounts for Portland-based Downstream, which creates digitally augmented branded environments for business, sports, and education clients around the world.

Homer Williams, instrumental in the development of Portland neighborhoods Forest Heights, the Pearl District, and the South Waterfront, is still active in real estate. He also has turned his attention to Portland's homeless population. In 2016 he started Harbor of Hope, which has led to a 100-bed shelter on Northwest Naito Parkway, a program of laundry and shower trucks offering free hygiene services, and Home Share Oregon, which matches homeowners with home seekers in need of affordable housing.

After experiencing a health crisis requiring multiple heart surgeries, former Dharma Bums singer/guitarist **Jeremy Wilson** was grateful to friends and fans who raised money to help him during his treatment and recovery. So much so that Wilson started the Jeremy Wilson Foundation (thejwf.org) to assist local musicians — who generally are independent contractors — during health-related challenges. Since the foundation began in 2010, it has awarded nearly 500 financial aid grants to music industry workers.

Acknowledgments

Thanks to Emily Brew, Jen Lewandowski, and Sandy Lyon for their great editing and even greater friendship.

And to the caregivers at the Franz Cancer Clinic and St. Vincent Medical Center in Portland, for keeping me here.

References

Introduction: A Golden Age For Creativity

Brooks, Karen. Interviewed by the author. January 8, 2023.

Cloepfil, Brad. Interviewed by the author. January 6, 2023.

Hicks, Bob. Interviewed by the author. January 10, 2023.

Schreiber, Cory. Interviewed by the author.
October 6, 2022.

Foster, Bill. Interviewed by the author. September 13, 2022.

Sandstrom, Steve. Interviewed by the author.
May 25, 2023.

Savinar, Tad. Interviewed by the author.
December 15, 2022.

Edmunds, Kristy. Interviewed by the author.
October 27, 2022.

Flaccus, Gillian. "Vera Katz, 3-term mayor of Portland who helped shape Oregon city into 'hipster haven,' dies at 84" *The Washington Post.* December 13, 2017.

Chapter 1: An Invitation to All

Erickson, Steve. "Crowd hits bricks for Pioneer Square's grand opening" *The Oregonian.* April 7, 1984.

Gragg, Randy A. and Alverson, Audrey. "Pioneering the Square" Presented by Portland Spaces. Thesqarepdx. org/uploads/2019/05/Pioneering-the-Square-Exhibit.pdf. May 2005.

Foster, Bill. Interviewed by the author. September 13, 2022.

Hyde, Cameron. Interviewed by the author. April 17, 2023.

1972 Downtown Plan. Retrieved from Portland.gov.

Heinz, Spencer. "5 Pioneer Square finalists set"
Oregon Journal. April 1, 1980.

Hayakawa, Alan R. "In the natural order of things"
The Oregonian. April 1, 1984.

Griffin, Anna. "Pioneer Courthouse Square at 30: 'Portland's
Living Room' has lasted because of its simplicity, continued
use" *The Oregonian.* April 4, 2014.

O'Neill, Patrick. "Ceremony in square eulogizes designer"
The Oregonian. October 14, 1985.

Chapter 2: Portland Gets Its Star

Simmons, Bill. "Let's go to the tape" *ESPN.com.* July 2, 2012.

Wolman, David. "Meet the Man Who Reinvented Nike,
Seduced Adidas, and Helped Make Portland the Sports Gear
Capital of the World" *Portland Monthly.* June 13, 2016.

Hehir, Jason (Director). "The Last Dance (Episode 5)."
Co-produced by ESPN Films and Netflix. First aired
May 3, 2020.

Peter, Josh, "Error Jordan: Key figures still argue
over who was responsible for Nike deal" *USA Today.*
September 30, 2015.

Schaefer, Rob. "How Spot-Bilt" nearly landed Michael Jordan
sneaker endorsement over Nike." *NBCsportschicago.com.*
May 5, 2020.

DePaula, Nick. "'Air' takes leaps but stays true to
Nike's actual chase of Michael Jordan" *Andscape.com.*
April 14, 2023.

Miller, Julie. "Air: The Real Sonny Vaccaro on Matt Damon,
Michael Jordan, and Shoe-Biz Heartbreak" *Vanity Fair.*
April 7, 2023

"Banned" 30-second commercial produced by Chiat/Day for
Nike. 1985.

Chapter 3: One Tough Campaign

Borders, Bill. Interviewed by the author. July 26, 2022.

Boyle, Gert with Tymchuk, Kerry. "One Tough Mother" *WestWinds Press.* April 1, 2005.

Steen, Margaret. "Columbia Sportswear: An American success story" *Family Business Magazine.* November 10, 2011.

Chapter 4: Something's Brewing

Ockert, Karl. Interviewed by the author. August 24, 2022.

McMenamin, Brian. Interviewed by the author. August 25, 2022.

Dunlop, Pete. "How Coors and Democratic Politicians almost killed Oregon beer" *Williamette Week.* June 16, 2015.

Woodward, Bob and Bennett, Laurel. "The History of Oregon Beer" *1859 Magazine.* January 1, 2010.

Yaeger, Brian. "Beer Guide 2013: An Oral History of the Widmer Hefeweizen" *Willamette Week.* March 19, 2013.

Edmunson-Morton, Tiah. "Kurt and Rob Widmer oral history interview" *Voices of Northwest Brewing Oral History Collection by Oregon State University.* May 10, 2014.

Edmunson-Morton, Tiah. "Fred Bowman oral history interview" *Voices of Northwest Brewing Oral History Collection by Oregon State University.* March 11, 2015.

Alworth, Jeff. "The Widmer Way: How Two Brothers Led Portland's Craft Beer Revolution" *Ooligan Press.* March 26, 2019.

Chapter 5: An Appetite for Change

Brooks, Karen. Interviewed by the author. January 8, 2023.

Higgins, Greg. Interviewed by the author. September 2, 2022.

Brooks, Karen. "Oregon's Cuisine of the Rain: From Lush Farm Foods to Regional Recipes" *Hachette Books.* March 20, 1993.

Brooks, Karen. "Restaurant of the Year: The Heathman Restaurant & Bar" *The Oregonian.* October 30, 1988.

Brooks, Karen. "Wine Snobs, Moody Bastards and Game Hens: Inside the Vat and Tonsure" *Portland Monthly.* August 15, 2016.

Dwan, Lois, "Portland's Culinary Isolationists" *Los Angeles Times.* May 18, 1986.

Chapter 6: Art Is On the Move

Kochs, Bob. Interviewed by the author. August 31, 2022.

Leach, Elizabeth. Interviewed by the author. October 28, 2022.

Black, Barbara. Interviewed by the author. September 14, 2022.

Gragg, Randy. "The Arlene Effect" *Portland Monthly.* April 27, 2017.

Vondersmith, Jason. *"First Lady of Portland Arts" Portland Tribune.* April 14, 2020.

Johnson, Barry. "First Thursday has arrived at last" *The Oregonian.* September 26, 1986.

Nicholas, Jonathan. *"PDX hit by art attack"* The Oregonian. February 9, 1987.

Chapter 7: Success from the Ground Up

Riswold, Jim. Interviewed by the author. August 16, 2022.

Foster, Bill. Interviewed by the author. September 13, 2022.

Wieden, Dan. Communications Council and AWARD lunch. Sydney, Australia. March 2015.

Brown, John. *Marketing Immortals.* June 20, 2011.

Chapter 8: A Stage for Authors

Prowda, Sherry. Interviewed by the author. May 3, 2023.

La Point, Peggy. "The Portland 50. Julie Mancini podcast interview" *101.9 KINK-FM.* January 30, 2019.

Pintarich, Paul. "Lecture series serves up cultural feast for Portland" *The Oregonian.* September 12, 1989.

Johnson, Barry. "Words matter: Who founded Literary Arts and who didn't" *Oregon ArtsWatch.* November 17, 2014.

"Past seasons" *Literary-arts.org*

Wolfe, Tom. "The Copper Goddess" *Newsweek.* July 14, 1986.

Chapter 9: Brands and Bands Come Together

Champ, Janet. Interviewed by the author. September 22, 2022.

Bedbury, Scott. Interviewed by the author. December 16, 2022.

"Can We Talk?" Print ad for Nike in *The Oregonian.* August 6, 1987.

Hilburn, Robert. "Beatles sue Nike over use of song" *Los Angeles Times.* July 29, 1987.

Rea, Stephen. "Advertisers find pop tunes perfect pitches." *Knight-Ridder News Service in The Oregonian.* August 20, 1987.

Ripatrazone, Nick. "Story Behind Nike's Controversial 1987 'Revolution' Commercial" *Rolling Stone.* February 22, 2017.

Beer, Jeff. "Thirty Years Later, The Story Behind Nike's Iconic 'Revolution'" *Fast Company.* March 31, 2017.

Rea, Stephen. "Advertisers find pop tunes perfect pitches." *Knight-Ridder News Service in The Oregonian.* August 20, 1987.

Chapter 10: Beer Goes to the Theater

McMenamin, Brian. Interviewed by the author. August 25, 2022.

Mission Theater and Pub history, McMenamins.com

Myers, Chris. "Movie house, saloon open in former church" *The Oregonian.* July 1, 1987.

"Barons of Brew" *The Oregonian.* February 19, 1995.

Edmunson-Morton, Tiah. McMenamins. *The Oregon Encyclopedia.*

Chapter 11: An Exciting Time for Art

Leach, Elizabeth. Interviewed by the author. January 23, 2023.

Rauschenberg, Christopher. Interviewed by the author. February 17, 2023.

Savinar, Tad. Interviewed by the author. December 15, 2022.

Jahn, Jeff. "Mel Katz has the last laugh" *Portlandart.net.* August 28, 2009.

"Twenty-Seven Installations' By Portland Center For The Visual Arts. *Publication Studio.* 2009.

Plagens, Peter. "Selections from the PCVA Archive" *Yale Union.* May 7-July 30, 2011.

Portlandgridproject.com

Chapter 12: Chaos Strikes Gold

Bedbury, Scott. Interviewed by the author. December 16, 2022.

Wieden, Dan. "Words from Wieden" *WKLondon.com.* February 18, 2005.

"Nike (1987) — Just Do It" *Creative Review.*

Bedbury, Scott. "Happy Birthday, Just Do It" *Medium.com.* August 21, 2018.

Brinckman, Jonathan. "Nike's 'Just Do It' slogan celebrates 20 years" *The Oregonian.* July 18, 2008.

Conlon, Jerome. "The Brand Brief Behind Nike's Just Do It Campaign" *Branding Strategy Insider.* August 2015.

Pray, Doug (Director). "Art & Copy" Documentary film released on August 21, 2009.

Chapter 13: A Festival of Beer

Ockert, Karl. Interviewed by the author. August 24, 2022.

Foyston, John. "In a well-quaffed crowd" *The Oregonian.* July 24, 1988.

"Who's who" The Oregonian. July 19, 1988.

Foyston, John. "The state of beer" *The Oregonian.* July 28, 2000.

Foyston, John. "Brewer's festival aged to perfection" *The Oregonian.* July 17, 2015.

Chapter 14: Pearl 1: A Land of Opportunity

Solheim, Al. Interviewed by author. August 31, 2022.

Savinar, Tad. Interviewed by the author. December 15, 2022.

Leach, Elizabeth. Interviewed by the author. October 28, 2022.

Eichinger, Martin. Interviewed by author. May 31, 2023.

Rauschenberg, Christopher. Interviewed by the author. February 17, 2023.

Edmunds, Kristy. Interviewed by the author. October 27, 2022.

Williams, Homer. Interviewed by author. September 21, 2022.

"Last Place in the Downtown Plan" *American Institute of Architects Regional-Urban Design Assistance Team.* May 1983.

Boule, Margie. "Pearl District's namesake was a jewel of a woman" *The Oregonian.* April 14, 2002.

Johnson, Bruce. "The Pearl District: Placemaking From The Ground Up" *Pearl Light Publishing.* July 26, 2022.

Chapter 15: It's Gotta Be the Ads

Riswold, Jim. Interviewed by the author. August 16, 2022.

Horton, Jay. "The Coolest Sneaker of the Last Year Exists Because a Portlander Wanted To Meet Bugs Bunny" *Willamette Week.* January 24, 2017.

Eisenberg, Jeff. "Iconic Sports Commercials: Michael Jordan and Mars Blackmon" *Yahoo Sports.* July 16, 2019.

Halberstam, David. "Playing For Keeps: Michael Jordan and the World He Made" *Random House.* February 1, 2000.

Chapter 16: The Power of Anti-Suggestion

Borders, Bill. Interviewed by the author. July 26, 2022.

Rothenberg, Randall. "Second Shoe Drops for Image Ads" *New York Times.* February 10, 1989.

White, George. "Shoe Maker Shuns Consumers With Vices: New Avia Ads Put Smokers on the Run" *Los Angeles Times.* February 17, 1989.

Chapter 17: Pearl 2: Art's Early Adopters

Black, Barbara. Interviewed by the author. September 14, 2022.

Edmunds, Kristy. Interviewed by the author. October 27, 2022.

Solheim, Al. Interviewed by author. August 31, 2022.

Gragg, Randy. Interviewed by author. November 11, 2022.

Gragg, Randy. "Portland loses heart of arts" *The Oregonian.* June 22, 1995.

Johnson, Barry. "Goodbye to the great, good gallery" *The Oregonian.* July 16, 1995.

Chapter 18: The World Was Moving

Blashfield Jim. Interviewed by the author. May 22, 2022.

Marsland, Melissa. Interviewed by the author. May 9, 2022.

Waritz, Rick. Interviewed by the author. May 25, 2022.

Johnson, Barry. "Jim Blashfield: And He Was" *Oregon ArtsWatch.* October 24, 2012.

"Video director zooms in on creative realities" *Associated Press.* December 24, 1989.

"Michael Jackson's 20 Greatest Videos: The Stories Behind the Vision" *Rolling Stone.* June 24, 2014.

Chapter 19: Bo's Moment to Remember

Riswold, Jim. Interviewed by the author. August 16, 2022.

Bedbury, Scott. Interviewed by the author. December 16, 2022.

Pearlman, Jeff. "The Last Folk Hero: The Life and Myth of Bo Jackson" *Mariner Books.* October 25, 2022.

Banks, Alec. "Behind the Swoosh: The Anatomy of Nike's 'Bo Knows' Campaign" *Highsnobiety.* July 15, 2014.

Wieden, Dan. "Words from Wieden" *WKLondon.com.* February 18, 2005.

"Topic of the Times: If the Shoe Doesn't Fit" *The New York Times.* February 15, 1989.

Chapter 20: The Streets Have Their Names

Leopold, Todd. "The Simpsons' Comedy Tree" *CNN.com.* December 14, 2009.

De La Roca, Claudia. "Matt Groening Reveals the Location of the Real Springfield" *Smithsonian Magazine. May 2012.*

"The Simpsons Archive" *Simpsonsarchive.com*

Chapter 21: Portland Hits Its Stride

Leach, Elizabeth. Interviewed by the author.
October 28, 2022.

Gomez, Stephen. Interviewed by the author. July 20, 2022.

Thompson, Gordon. Interviewed by the author.
August 18, 2022.

Levy, Shawn. Interviewed by the author.
December 8, 2022.

Peck, Gary. Interviewed by the author. September 23, 2022.

Champ, Janet. Interviewed by the author.
September 22, 2022.

"Portland Metro Area Population 1950–2023" *Macrotrends.net*

"When was Portland's best decade" *The Oregonian.*
August 1, 2016.

Dundas, Zach. "1999" *Willamette Week.* March 8, 2005.

Chapter 22: Zefiro Starts a Scene

Carey, Bruce. Interviewed by the author.
September 12, 2022.

Gomez, Stephen. Interviewed by the author. July 20, 2022.

Thompson, Gordon. Interviewed by the author.
August 18, 2022.

Schreiber, Cory. Interviewed by the author.
October 6, 2022.

Higgins, Greg. Interviewed by the author.
September 2, 2022.

Brooks, Karen and Sarasohn, David. "Restaurant of the Year 1991: Zefiro." *The Oregonian.* October 27, 1991.

Porter, Roger. "Sept. 14, 1990: A New Restaurant Opens at the Corner of Northwest 21st Avenue and Glisan Street..." *Willamette Week.* November 4, 2014.

Brooks, Karen. "How Zefiro Changed Everything for Portland's Food Scene" *Portland Monthly.* August 15, 2016.

Hodgkinson, Mike. "Monique Siu: the Chinese-American chef who put Portland on the culinary map" *South China Morning Post.* July 11, 2019.

Chapter 23: Field of Exceeded Dreams

McMenamin, Brian. Interviewed by the author. August 25, 2022.

Edgefield history, *McMenamins.com*

Ruble, Web. "Historic poor farm gets new lease on life" *The Oregonian.* May 31, 1993.

Hill, Jim. "Barons of Brew" *The Oregonian.* February 19, 1995.

Chapter 24: Nike's Kind of Town

Thompson, Gordon. Interviewed by the author. August 18, 2022.

Bedbury, Scott. Interviewed by the author. December 16, 2022.

Champ, Janet. Interviewed by the author. September 22, 2022.

Hamburg, Ken. "Nike Town Meant to Wow" *The Oregonian.* November 21, 1990.

Hannon, Kerry. "The 1992 Store of the Year" *Money.* December 1, 1991.

Brettman, Allan. "NikeTown Portland to close forever on Friday" *The Oregonian.* October 27, 2011.

Pine, Joseph and Gilmore, James. "Welcome to the Experience Economy" *Harvard Business Review.* July–August 1998.

Buchman, Lorne. "The untold story of how Apple built a retail empire on trial and error" *Fast Company.* October 14, 2021.

Chapter 25: It's a Foot Race

Thompson, Gordon. Interviewed by the author.
August 18, 2022.

James, Brent. Interviewed by the author. August 1, 2022.

Reilly, Jim. Interviewed by the author. October 27, 2022.

Katinsky, Jon and Sheri. Interviewed by the author.
January 28, 2023.

Peck, Gary. Interviewed by the author. September 23, 2022.

Knight, Phil. "Shoe Dog: A Memoir by the Creator of Nike"
Simon & Schuster. April 26, 2016.

Bates, Tom. "Mr. Big: Rob Strasser is engineering the second
coming of Adidas." *The Oregonian.* September 26, 1993.

Wolman, David. "Meet the Man Who Reinvented Nike,
Seduced Adidas, and Helped Make Portland the Sports Gear
Capital of the World" *Portland Monthly.* June 13, 2016.

Chapter 26: Pearl 3: A Place to Call Home

Foster, Bill. Interviewed by the author. September 23, 2022.

Thomas, Debbie. Interviewed by the author.
October, 4, 2022.

Peters, Keith. Interviewed by the author. July 13, 2022.

"Carroll to convert Chown Pella warehouse
to condominiums" *Portland Business Journal.*
September 22, 1995.

Dunham, Elisabeth. "Lofty Goals" *The Oregonian.*
April 9, 1998.

Chapter 27: Please Welcome to the Stage

Hughley, Marty. Interviewed by the author. July 11, 2023.

Wilson. Jeremy. Interviewed by the author.
August 23, 2003.

Hughley, Marty. "So long, Satyricon" *The Oregonian.*
October 17, 2010.

Schultz, Curt. "Rewind on Dharma Bums blur"
The Oregonian. February 19, 2010.

Ham, Robert. "The Dream Really Was Alive"
Portland Mercury. August 22, 2018.

Clarke, Cary. "Our Town Could Be Your Life"
Portland Mercury. February 18, 2010.

Foyston, John. "Honoring a Portland Music Icon"
The Oregonian. February 24, 2007.

Perry, Douglas. "Billy Rancher raced toward '80s stardom,
until tragedy struck" The Oregonian. August 12, 2019.

Tomlinson, Stuart. "Cool'r is Heating Up" *The Oregonian.*
January 29, 1989.

Tomlinson, Stuart. "Fourth Time Proves Charm For Opening
Of Big Tour As Band Balances Getting Pumped Up, Playing It
Cool." *The Oregonian.* July 22, 1990.

Hughley, Marty. "Crazy 8s Fold the Cards, Deck"
The Oregonian. December 25, 1994.

Singer, Matthew. "The Last of The Sad Bastards"
Willamette Week. October 15, 2023.

Young, Chris, "Portraits of Portland Music"
Vortex Music Magazine. May 5, 2014.

Wright, Craig. "The Replacements — Portland, 1987.
Was it the band's worst show ever?" *The Daily Emerald.*
April 7, 2015.

Singer, Matthew. "Swingin' Party" *Willamette Week.*
April 7, 2015.

Chapter 28: Putting Portland on the Table

Higgins, Greg. Interviewed by the author.
September 2, 2022.

Schreiber, Cory. Interviewed by the author.
October 6, 2022.

Chapter 29: A Welcome Return

Schreiber, Cory. Interviewed by the author. October 6, 2022.

Brooks, Karen. "Restaurant of the Year: Wildwood" *The Oregonian.* October 22, 1995.

Chapter 30: A Food City Rises

Higgins, Greg. Interviewed by the author. September 2, 2022.

Miller, Bryan. "Inspired By the Produce Of Portland" *The New York Times.* July 9, 1995.

Paley, Kimberly and Vitaly. "The Paley's Place Cookbook: Recipes and stories from the Pacific Northwest" *Ten Speed Press.* October 1, 2008.

Rommelmann, Nancy. "Interview: Chef Philippe Boulot" *Portland Food and Drink* April 3, 2006.

Chapter 31: Changing the Ad Game

Perlman, Hank. Interviewed by the author. January 31, 2023.

Champ, Janet. Interviewed by the author. September 22, 2022.

Elliott, Stuart. "Jocks and jokes set a theme for campaigns chosen as the decades best advertising" *The New York Times.* December 15, 1999.

Rubin, Mike. "The Straw That Stirs the Shtick" *The New York Times.* October 18, 1998.

"ESPN and Wieden & Kennedy: A Look Back at One of the Most Storied Creative Partnerships in Marketing" *Ad Age.* January 27, 2017.

Chapter 32: Dining With a Twist of Cool

Carey, Bruce. Interviewed by the author. September 12, 2022.

Cloepfil, Brad. Interviewed by the author. January 6, 2023.

Brooks, Karen. "Putting the sauce in the box" *The Oregonian.* November 29, 1996.

Church, Foster. "He imports a cosmopolitan flavor" *The Oregonian.* June 8, 1997.

Perry, Sara. "Ambassador of eating well" *The Oregonian.* August 3, 1997.

Sarasohn, David. "Restaurant of the Year: Saucebox" *The Oregonian.* April 10, 1998.

Hamlin, Suzanne. "An Oregon Trail of Portland Treats" *The New York Times.* June 28, 1998.

Chapter 33: A New Voice Emerges

Champ, Janet. Interviewed by the author. September 22, 2022.

Berger, Warren. "They know Bo" *The New York Times Magazine.* November 1, 1990.

Mitchell, Jann. "Janet Champ: Instinct for Inspiration" *The Oregonian.* October 23, 1994.

Video. "30 years of creative chaos, with Dan Wieden & Sir John Hegarty" *Cannes Lions.* 2012.

Schenck, Ernie. "60 years of blockbuster culture shapers and the advertising that changed everything" *Communication Arts.*

Brettman, Allan. "Nike, Wieden + Kennedy women's ad campaign broke new ground 20 years ago" *The Oregonian.* April 13, 2015.

Huval, Rebecca. "Selling Sneakers with Feminist Poetry: An Interview with Janet Champ" *Feminism.* April 27, 2015.

Chapter 34: A Leap Forward for the Arts

Edmunds, Kristy. Interviewed by the author. October 27, 2022.

Gragg, Randy. Interviewed by author. November 11, 2022.

Gragg, Randy. "PICA in the Pearl" *The Oregonian.*
February 25, 2000.

Row, D.K. "Ephemeral Adventures" *The Oregonian.*
June 10, 2005.

Chapter 35: This Place Was Hopping

Ockert, Karl. Interviewed by the author. August 24, 2022.

Geist, Gary. Interviewed by the author. July 19, 2023.

Yaeger, Brian. "Beer Guiide 2014: An Oral History
of BridgePort India Pale Ale" *Williamette Week.*
February 4, 2014.

Foyston, John. "BridgePort IPA Day toasts the world
championship beer" *The Oregonian.* August 4, 2000.

Chapter 36: Creativity Pays

Sandstrom, Steve. Interviewed by the author on
May 25, 2023.

Potestio, Steve. Interviewed by the author on
June 14, 2023.

Chitwood, Ken. Interviewed by the author on July 12, 2023.

Waritz, Rick. Interviewed by the author. May 25, 2022.

Read, Richard. "Portland Tea Savant Steven Smith,
co-founder of Tazo, Stash and Smith Teamaker, dies at 65"
The Oregonian. March 23, 2015.

Chapter 37: More Brewers Pour In

Geist, Gary. Interviewed by the author. July 19, 2023.

Scott, Jackie. "Something's brewing Saturday" *The Oregonian.*
April 20, 1995.

Foyston, John. "Winter ales, ales, the gang's all here"
The Oregonian. December 6, 1996.

Foyston, John. "Majoring in beer" *The Oregonian.*
August 22, 1997.

Francis, Mike. "Craft brewing loses its buzz." *The Oregonian.* December 30, 1997.

Nkruma, Wade. "Changed Oktoberfest returns to Oaks Park" *The Oregonian.* May4, 1998.

Foyston, John. "Sample the sudsational at the Spring Beet Fest" *The Oregonian.* April 28, 2000.

Meunier, Andre. "Hair of the Dog brewery, taproom to close as legendary founder Alan Sprints is retiring" *The Oregonian.* February 14, 2022.

Meunier, Andre. "10 old-school Portland brewpubs that lunched the city's beer scene" *The Oregonian.* October 26, 2018.

Chapter 38: Reuse, Remake, And Refill

McMenamin, Brian. Interviewed by the author. August 25, 2022.

Cloepfil, Brad. Interviewed by the author. January 6, 2023.

Bedbury, Scott. Interviewed by the author. December 16, 2022.

Foyston, John. "The Crystal Glows Again" *The Oregonian.* October 22, 1995.

Foyston, John. "Crystal Rocks Anew" *The Oregonian.* February 18, 1997.

Hortsch, Dan. "From blackboard to brews" *The Oregonian.* October 16, 1997.

Chapter 39: What A Ride

Hatfield, Tinker. Interviewed by the author. September 12, 2023.

DePaula, Nick. "New Air Jordan 3 honors the designer who saved Nike" *ESPN.* March 22, 2018.

Chapter 40: Pearl 4: An Expanded Vision

Williams, Homer. Interviewed by author.
September 21, 2022.

Gragg, Randy. Interviewed by author. November 11, 2022.

Thomas, Debbie. Interviewed by the author.
October, 4, 2022.

Levy, Shawn. Interviewed by the author.
December 8, 2022.

"River District: A Development Plan for Portland's North Downtown" 1994.

Duin, Steve. "Homer Williams develops opportunity with wit, charm" *The Oregonian.* July, 1998.

Jaquiss, Nigel. "Homer's Odyssey" *Willamette Week.*
July 29, 2003.

Johnson, Bruce. "The Pearl District: Placemaking From The Ground Up" *Pearl Light Publishing.* July 26, 2022.

Chapter 41: One Call Changed It All

Cloepfil, Brad. Interviewed by the author. January 6, 2023.

Edmunds, Kristy. Interviewed by the author.
October 27, 2022.

Gragg, Randy. "Ice house comes in from the cold thanks to pioneering partners" *The Oregonian.* April 12, 1997.

Gragg, Randy. "New art for a new Portland" *The Oregonian.*
July 5, 1998.

Gragg, Randy. "Cinderella Complex" *The Oregonian.*
November 14, 1999.

Lieber, Ron. "Creative Space" *Fast Company.*
December 31, 2000.

Afterword: So, What's Next?

Meehan, Brian. "Oregonians welcome 2000" *The Oregonian.* January 1, 2000.

Timeline. "Portland's Living Room" *Thesquarepdx.com.*

"Awards Nominees and Winners" *Emmys.com.*

Brick, Michael. "A Shoe Rivalry Extends to Oregon Office Sites" *The New York Times.* December 11, 2002.

Russell, Michael. "The birth of a scene" *MIX, The Oregonian.* April 2012.

"Best New Chefs 2009: Naomi Pomeroy" *Food & Wine.*

"2016 Oregon Craft Beer By The Numbers" *Brewpublic.com.* April 20, 2017.

Miller, Claire Cain. "Will Portland Always Be a Retirement Community for the Young?" *The New York Times Magazine.* September 16, 2018.

About the Author

 In 40 years as a professional writer, Barry Locke has traveled from the Taj Mahal to the Berlin Wall. He has written for newspapers, magazines, and websites. He has worked in marketing communications, employee communications, and advertising. He knows how to tell a story.

In his first book, *Portland Renaissance*, Barry captures the stories that elevated Portland from the mid-1980s through the 1990s, sharing insights and anecdotes from those who played prominent roles, and examining the conditions that led to the city's resurgence.

Barry lives with his wife, Kim, in Portland, where every day is just a little better when their two grown sons remember to call home.

Printed in the USA
CPSIA information can be obtained
at www.ICGtesting.com
JSHW072129101123
51839JS00008B/34